More Than We Can Imagine: A Practical Guide to the Holy Spirit

Dick Robinson

PRESS

More Than We Can Imagine:
A Practical Guide to the Holy Spirit
by Dick Robinson

Printed in the United States of America

ISBN 978-1-60477-848-9

Dick Robinson's website is www.healingourhearts.org. This website describes the personal, one-on-one ministry he has been involved in since the late 1970s. See Isaiah 61:1–3.

www.xulonpress.com

ACKNOWLEDGEMENTS

The Lord arranged for my missionary friend Paul Shots-berger, in Kiev, Ukraine, to invite me to come and teach a Theology of the Holy Spirit course to Ukrainian pastors in 2004. My preparation of materials to give them during the course was the beginning of this book. A year after returning, I was reviewing what I had written and felt a strong leading of the Holy Spirit to write a book about Him for the blessing of anyone who would read it. That material needed a lot of work. I thank the Lord and my friend Paul for these beginning steps. I thank the Lord for His sustaining encouragement during the several years of writing the book.

My good friend Walt Pilcher has prayed for this project over these several years, and has read drafts of nearly all the chapters. He understood what I was trying to do. At my request, he has brought some very helpful suggestions that have enhanced the book. For the spending of himself for this book I am very grateful.

Over the last year or so I have asked several pastor friends to read my manuscript and tell me what they thought. These pastors have invested in the book through their time spent with the manuscript, and through their encouragement to me. I thank Bill Hyer, Jim Martin, Joe McKechnie, Doug Murphy and Howard Shockley.

The Lord led me to a wonderful sister in the Lord who is a professional editor. Donna Rees has brought her wonderful understanding of how our English language should be presented on the page to this book. I used to think I knew about these things. She has done a masterful job, as unto the Lord. For her excellent professional work and caring encouragement I give great thanks.

To my wife Carrie I give thanks for her understanding and patience as I left her for the keyboard for so many hours. She continued to encourage me as I sought to follow the leading of the Lord. After forty-two years of marriage, she knew I would come back to her. I thank God for her.

March 2008

Table of Contents

	Introduction............................ ix
CHAPTER ONE:	My Introduction to the Holy Spirit......................... 11
CHAPTER TWO:	The Nature of His Being......... 15
CHAPTER THREE:	His Divinity and His Function in the Trinity 19
CHAPTER FOUR:	His Personality....................... 29
CHAPTER FIVE:	His Part in Regeneration......... 33
CHAPTER SIX:	His Indwelling of the Believer............................... 43
CHAPTER SEVEN:	His Part in Illumination and Guidance 47
CHAPTER EIGHT:	His Part in Sanctification 57

CHAPTER NINE: His Desire for Fellowship.......63

CHAPTER TEN: His Fruit.................................71

CHAPTER ELEVEN: His Gifts................................81

CHAPTER TWELVE: His Desire to Use
                     Believers in Ministry..........91

CHAPTER THIRTEEN: His Omnipresence and His
                     Manifest Presence..............97

CHAPTER FOURTEEN: Baptized With the
                     Holy Spirit.......................103

CHAPTER FIFTEEN: Experiencing the Manifest
                     Presence of God...............119

CHAPTER SIXTEEN: More Than We Can
                     Imagine 131

Introduction

I write this book because I believe a simple guide to the Person and work of the Holy Spirit should be available to all Christians. It is my hope that pastors and teachers will find it useful as a tool with which to teach their people.

There are several good books about being baptized with the Holy Spirit and about the gifts of the Spirit, but I have never found a simple, practical, and readable guide that explains just who the Holy Spirit is, how He works in us, and how He functions as part of the Trinity. My observation is that most Christians have little or no vision of themselves being used by the Holy Spirit, empowered by Him, bringing great blessings to the Lord's people as well as non-Christians, and bringing blessing and honor to the Name of our Lord, Jesus. I want to encourage vision and expectation. So now I offer this practical guide to the Holy Spirit based on my study and over thirty-seven years of experience as a Christian who has sought to be led and empowered by the Holy Spirit, twenty-three of those years serving as a pastor.

In this guide, you will learn who the Holy Spirit is and how He is a member of the Trinity. You will learn about His personality and how He wants to fellowship with you. You will read about how the Spirit wants to guide you and to work through you, with His power and wisdom, in your service to

God. I will share some of the miracles I have been privileged to witness or to be a part of, as well as some of the many blessings I have enjoyed because of my personal fellowship with Him. It is my prayer that as a result of reading this book, you will gain more confidence in seeking and walking with the Holy Spirit and in telling others about Him.

I have included practical applications, explanations, and examples wherever possible. In the hands of Christians who are interested in getting to know God's Holy Spirit as a Person, this little book should open up understanding of His goals, His ways, and His great desire to bless us as servants of the Most High God. The Holy Spirit is the One sent by God. He is supernatural and He does supernatural things that affect people and the world in which we live. An example is the time I had a lump the size of a navy bean in my right upper arm. I had scheduled surgery to have it removed, but then I asked some Christians to pray for my healing. During the prayer time, I sensed that the Lord was taking care of it. In a few days it had shrunk to half its original size. I cancelled the surgery. In ten days, it was totally gone. That was more than a year ago.

It is my desire to cultivate in each reader a desire to know the Holy Spirit and to seek His guidance and power in their lives, as well as to motivate each reader to step forth in His wisdom and His power to bless others as they are being directed by Him.

Please note that in this book, names have been changed in order to protect pastoral confidentiality.

Dick Robinson

CHAPTER ONE

My Introduction to the Holy Spirit

I grew up in an unchurched home in Los Angeles, California. I was saved in November of 1970, at the age of 32, while living in the San Francisco area. After years of struggling against the gentle, loving, but insistent wooing of the Holy Spirit, I finally surrendered to the awesome goodness and majesty of the Lord Jesus Christ. I was born again, and the Holy Spirit took up residence inside me, never to leave. He was ready to begin guiding and empowering my life immediately, as I learned to let Him have control.

There were several immediate changes in my life. The Bible became very important to me, although I had never read it before. I felt compelled to find a church that my family could attend, where the Bible was believed and taught. We found one near our home, in Walnut Creek, California. Within a year, at the direction of the Lord, we moved from the San Francisco Bay area to Atlanta and found another solid evangelical church.

I was eager to learn, so I became involved in a weekly small group Bible study that met during the evening and a men's breakfast group that met every week. My wife and I attended a couples' Sunday School class, and after about two years I was sharing responsibility for the leadership of that class with several other men my age. It was a Presbyterian church, and soon I was elected to serve as a deacon. I was really busy for the Lord!

This church preached the Gospel faithfully. Every year they raised a lot of money for missions during a week-long conference. The people of this church were willing to give into God's Kingdom, and many were very active in the church activities. I saw people working hard for God. However, although they showed plenty of determination, I didn't see a whole lot of joy in them.

One Sunday morning, before the senior pastor began his sermon, I read the passage of Scripture that was referenced in the bulletin: Matthew 3:1–12. In verse 11, I read these words of John the Baptist: "As for me, I baptize you with water for repentance, but He who is coming after me is mightier than I, and I am not fit to remove His sandals; He will baptize you with the Holy Spirit and fire." I was very curious to learn about the Holy Spirit. I had been a Christian for four years and had never heard anyone teach on that subject. Perhaps there had been passing mention of Him, but no real instruction. And now here it was. I was finally going to receive teaching on the Holy Spirit.

The pastor read verses 1 through 10, skipped over verse 11, and then read verse 12.

I was shocked. Then I felt really disappointed, even angry. His selective avoidance of that verse of Scripture seemed almost dishonest, yet the senior pastor was reputed to be a godly man of great integrity. Why did he skip over verse 11?

I just had to find out. It seemed to me that this avoidance of verse 11 was quite bizarre and probably was motivated by some pretty strong feelings in the pastor. Wanting to avoid a potentially difficult moment with the pastor, I decided to ask some people who knew him well to see if they had an answer. They thought that he had skipped that verse probably because he wanted to avoid mention of being baptized with the Holy Spirit. He didn't want people asking him about it, and he didn't want to appear to endorse this idea, which seemed too "Pentecostal" for this particular church. I didn't know exactly what to make of all that, but it left me with a growing sense that something was missing from my Christian life.

Not long after that Jim, one of the church elders, approached me after the service one Sunday and invited me to have lunch with him. At lunch, Jim said he had observed me working very hard at being a good Christian, and he was concerned that I might be getting into "Christian burn-out." He had seen a number of new Christians who were very motivated and worked hard but then became worn out and even quite disillusioned.

What many people don't understand, he said, is that God has placed His Holy Spirit in us to *empower* us for the Christian life. God doesn't expect *us* to provide all the energy and strength, or even all the wisdom, that is needed in our lives as Christians. Jim reminded me that Jesus said His yoke is easy. I had to agree with him that I was getting a little tired and discouraged and needed something more.

Jim asked me to read Acts 1:1–8, where Jesus promised His disciples that they would soon be baptized with the Holy Spirit and that they would receive power. He told me that this promise of Jesus still applied to all those of us who are His followers today, including me. He encouraged me to get to know the Holy Spirit myself and to learn how to let Him guide and empower me. He explained that an intimate relationship with the Holy Spirit begins with surrender to Him. Jim pointed out that the Holy Spirit is the Spirit of Christ and that since I had trusted in Jesus Christ, I could trust the Holy Spirit as well.

I'm not sure where Jim learned about the Holy Spirit, but I am grateful to the Lord for enabling him to see my plight and for guiding him to come to my rescue with his counsel. It was the answer to the "something more" that I needed.

I followed Jim's advice, and my life has not been the same since then. Just a few years after that encounter with Jim, I felt called by God to become a pastor, and I went to seminary. The adventure of serving the Lord for over thirty years with the Holy Spirit in charge has been nothing short of miraculous and wonderful.

Over the years since then, I have seen how God's Holy Spirit is the subject of considerable controversy. The Evangelical and Pentecostal groups have different theologies about the Holy Spirit, and even within these groups there are differences. Many pastors and teachers simply want to avoid the controversy. Too often, this has resulted in a tragic lack of preaching and teaching about this very important subject in the Body of Christ. Many pastors and teachers who have been trying to avoid the controversy are sidestepping their responsibility to teach the Body of Christ about the Person of the Holy Spirit.

I was fortunate to learn fairly early in my Christian walk how important the Holy Spirit is, and I'm grateful to Him for all that He has done in my life. All Christians should be intimately acquainted with God's Holy Spirit and yielded to His guidance and power. We can be transformed by the Holy Spirit and be led and empowered by Him for service so that we and others whom we equip or whose lives we touch can walk in sweet fellowship with Him for all of their days.

CHAPTER TWO

The Nature of His Being

In order to understand the Holy Spirit, we must learn something about His nature. Our Lord Jesus declared that "God is spirit" (John 4:24). God is spirit in His entirety, as are all three Persons of the Godhead: Father, Son, and Holy Spirit. Jesus used the noun *spirit* to describe God, and therefore spirit has existence, though it does not consist of matter made of atoms.

In the Old Testament, the Hebrew word translated most often as *spirit* is the word *rûach*, and in the New Testament, the Greek word almost exclusively translated as *spirit* is the word *pneuma*. In both cases, in everyday usage, these words are understood to mean "air," "breath," or "spirit." God has chosen to use these two words in the Old and New Testaments to describe the third Person of His Trinity.

Among the very first words of the Bible, we see the word *rûach* used, as we read, ". . . And the Spirit of God was moving over the surface of the waters" (Genesis 1:2). Jesus used *pneuma* when referring to the Holy Spirit when He said, "The wind blows where it wishes and you hear the sound of it, but do not know where it comes from and where it is going; so is every one who is born of the Spirit" (John 3:8).

We can see from these two Scriptures that a spirit can act. As Scripture describes the actions of spirits, we learn that God holds them morally responsible. In order to be morally responsible, they must have the ability to think, feel, and choose. We find that Scripture describes the Holy Spirit, or the Spirit of God, as holy and godly, and evil spirits are described as evil.

Since Scripture declares that God is spirit, we understand that the Father is spirit, the Son is spirit, and the Holy Spirit is spirit. The Holy Spirit is God in the form of spirit, with a mind, will, and emotions. In Genesis 6:3, we learn that He has dealings with men: "My Spirit shall not strive with man forever . . . ."

After the Flood, which is described in Genesis 7 and 8, God began to relate to that group of people whom He called His own. After their captivity and release from Egypt, they wandered in the wilderness, and God instructed Moses to construct a sanctuary for Him, in the form of a tabernacle (Exodus 25:8–9). During its construction, God placed His Spirit upon Bezalel to give him skills in craftsmanship (Exodus 31:3). This is the Bible's first mention of a situation in which the Spirit of God directly affected one of God's people.

The occasion when the Spirit of the Lord first came upon King David is described in I Samuel 16:13: ". . . The Spirit of the Lord came mightily upon David from that day forward." After David's sin with Bathsheba, the Spirit of the Lord convicted him of that sin. David called out to God in a prayer of repentance, asking that the Holy Spirit not be taken from him. This plea is recorded in Psalm 51:11 and is the Old Testament's first use of the term *Holy Spirit*, in reference to the Spirit of God.

The Spirit of God is called the Holy Spirit to indicate both His nature and His operation. In His nature, He is absolutely holy and without sin or flaw, and He is the cause of holiness wherever it is found in creation. God's desire is to conform us to the image of the Son, as we can see in Romans 8:29. This process of conformity involves saving an unholy sinner and bringing holiness into his life through sanctification, an ongoing work of the Holy Spirit. The more we allow the holiness of the Holy Spirit to influence and change us, the more we become conformed to the image of the Son.

The life of John Newton, the writer of the well-known hymn "Amazing Grace," provides an excellent example of an individual who was saved and responded humbly to the Spirit's work in his life. Born in England in 1725, his mother died when he was quite young, and he went to sea with his father, who was a ship captain. John rebelled during his teen years and ended up becoming the servant of a slave trader who brutally abused him. John Newton became an angry and worldly young man. A friend of his father rescued him from that brutal situation, but John stayed in the slave trade, soon becoming the captain of his own slave trade ship.

While still in his early twenties, he was returning from a distant place when his ship was overtaken by a powerful and treacherous storm that threatened to sink the ship and crew. He cried out, "Lord, have mercy on us!" God intervened and spared his ship. At that time, John became aware of God's grace, and for the rest of his life he regarded that day as the day of his conversion. He described himself as a "wretch" who was saved by grace. Ultimately, he was ordained as a pastor in England and drew crowds who came to hear his passionate preaching. He wrote more than 280 hymns, as one means of expressing praise to the God who saved him. The Holy Spirit brought significant holiness to John Newton's life in the fifty-nine years following his conversion.

In the Holy Spirit's operation, He is powerful without limitation, and His wisdom is perfect. This equips the Spirit to carry out His purpose, which is to accomplish the will of God as it has been established in the Godhead. We see an example of the Holy Spirit's powerful operation in the way He arranged for Moses to be raised in the household of Egypt's Pharaoh and thus be particularly suited for the task of dealing with Pharaoh later, when the Holy Spirit worked miracles as God led His people out of Egypt. Because of the Spirit's nature and operation, He also is called the Comforter, the Helper, the Spirit of Truth, the Spirit of Wisdom, the Spirit of Peace, the Spirit of Love, and the Spirit of Glory.

Some people, of various persuasions, have taken the position that the Holy Spirit is simply the power, or force, of God. In this view, there is no awareness of God being involved as a Person in our lives. Instead, the term *Holy Spirit* is seen simply as a way of describing the operation of God in the earth, from afar. This view generally sees the operation of the Holy Spirit in a person's life as coming from outside the person. Even for many who are believers, the idea of the Holy Spirit operating from inside the person is very vague, or nonexistent. We will examine this point in greater depth later.

CHAPTER THREE

His Divinity and His Function in the Trinity

The issue of the divinity of the Holy Spirit is a critical one. If He is not God, then we do not have a Trinity in the Godhead; we would have only the Father and the Son.

Much Scripture testifies that the Holy Spirit is God. The Great Commission passage in Matthew 28:18–20 confirms that the Holy Spirit is a member of the Trinity: "... Baptizing them in the name of the Father and the Son and the Holy Spirit." This passage also affirms that the Holy Spirit is divine, because to baptize in the name of anyone or anything other than God would be idolatrous. In Acts 5:3–4, Peter said to Ananias, "Why has Satan filled your heart to lie to the Holy Spirit . . . ? . . . You have not lied to men, but to God." The Holy Spirit is God.

On the occasion when Isaiah saw the Lord high and lifted up, he said, "Then I heard the voice of the Lord . . . . He said, 'Go and tell this people, Keep on listening, but do not perceive'. . ." (Isaiah 6:8–9). Hundreds of years later, the Apostle Paul said, " 'The Holy Spirit rightly spoke through Isaiah the prophet to your fathers, saying, "Go to this people and say, 'You will keep on hearing, but will not understand;

and you will keep on seeing, but will not perceive . . .' " (Acts 28:25–26). Paul was quoting from the passage in Isaiah, and he understood that when Isaiah said he heard the voice of the Lord, he had heard the Holy Spirit speaking. The Holy Spirit was acting in a divine capacity, because He is divine. He is God.

As Jeremiah was prophesying the restoration of Israel, he said, " 'But this is the covenant which I will make with the house of Israel after those days,' declares the Lord, 'I will put My law within them, and on their heart I will write it . . .' " (Jeremiah 31:33). Centuries later, the author of Hebrews wrote, ". . . The Holy Spirit also bears witness to us; for after saying [or "after He said"], 'This is the covenant that I will make with them after those days, says the Lord: I will put My laws upon their heart, and upon their mind I will write them' " (Hebrews 10:15–16). The writer of Hebrews clearly understood that it was the Holy Spirit who spoke through Jeremiah. Since Jeremiah knew that it was the Lord speaking through him, we conclude that as the Holy Spirit was speaking, He was functioning in a divine capacity as the third Person of the Trinity. He was functioning as God.

The Holy Spirit functions in the Trinity, the Godhead, in complete unity with the Father and the Son. They are never at odds. They decide things in perfect unison. They have the same worldview, the same love for us, and the same hatred for evil. They have the same plan for redemption and the same plan for eternity.

The Persons of the Trinity—Father, Son, and Holy Spirit—make all decisions in total agreement. An example of their unity is recorded in Genesis 1:26: "Let Us make man in Our image . . . ." Each of the Persons of the Trinity plays a part in whatever is done by God. Our human, logical minds seem to want crystal clear definitions of things, but we must never allow our thinking to include the idea that there are three Gods. God is One, and at the same time He exists in three Persons. Our logical minds may not be able to comprehend this truth, but this is how God has described Himself in Scripture.

It does seem clear from Scripture that each Person has special responsibilities, all agreed upon by the Trinity. I like to think of it this way:

- The Father is the initiator of the overall plan.
- The Son is the One who creates. He is the Messiah and the Shepherd of God's people.
- The Holy Spirit performs the works of God in the earth.

Within that framework, without trying to cover all the possibilities, and recognizing that sometimes the responsibilities are shared or overlapping, I want to mention several major functions of each Person, which are delineated in Scripture.

The Father is the initiator of the overall plan. He has a Father-heart of love toward His creation. He said, "I have surely seen the affliction of My people who are in Egypt, and have given heed to their cry because of their taskmasters, for I am aware of their sufferings" (Exodus 3:7). He said, ". . . I will be their God, and they shall be My people" (Jeremiah 31:33). We are also told, "It is for discipline that you endure; God deals with you as with sons; for what son is there whom his father does not discipline?" (Hebrews 12:7).

It is from the Father that the Holy Spirit proceeds, though the Son also sends the Holy Spirit (John 15:26). The Holy Spirit is also called the Spirit of Christ (Romans 8:9). In addition to the fact that the Son has sent the Spirit, the Holy Spirit is called the Spirit of Christ because He has the same personality as Christ, the same goals, the same values, and the same love for people. Anyone who has trusted the Son can trust the Holy Spirit.

The Son is the One who creates, according to the plan of the Godhead. "All things came into being by Him; and apart from Him nothing came into being that has come into being" (John 1:3). "For in Him all things were created, both in the heavens and on earth, visible and invisible, whether thrones or dominions or rulers or authorities—all things have been created by Him and for Him" (Colossians 1:16). Now, from His position as ruler of the universe at the right hand of the Father, the Son sometimes moves by the Holy Spirit to do creative signs and wonders through the ministry of His people, such as the creation of skin, muscle, blood vessels, and nerves in the legs of the 40-year-old lame man who sat at the gate called Beautiful (Acts 3:1–8). After this creative miracle, the man who was lame from birth ran, leaping and jumping and praising God.

The Son is the Messiah (John 1:41) whose birth was prophesied seven hundred years earlier (Isaiah 9:6). As the Holy Spirit came upon Mary, she found herself with a child in her womb who was the Son of God (Luke 1:35). John the Baptist prophesied as he baptized Jesus, "Behold, the Lamb of God who takes away the sin of the world!" (John 1:29). In a few short years, Jesus would be crucified as the Lamb of God (Isaiah 53:7), as an atonement for our sin (Romans 3:21–26, 5:6–11). His resurrection verified that He is the Son of God and our Messiah (Romans 1:4). After His resurrection, He ascended to Heaven (Acts 1:9–11) and now sits at the right hand of the Father, reigning over the universe (Hebrews 10:11–13, I Corinthians 15:22–28).

When Jesus began His ministry among the Jewish people, He said He was the Good Shepherd (John 10:14). As Lord of the universe, He reigns as "the great Shepherd of the sheep through the blood of the eternal covenant, even Jesus our Lord" (Hebrews 13:20; see also I Peter 2:21–25). He wants us to acknowledge that we are His sheep and that He is our wonderful and perfect Shepherd (see John 10:14–16). Sheep know who their "lord" is . . . their shepherd. Unless we regularly acknowledge Him as our great Shepherd, we tend to be self-sufficient and independent, which leads to our disobedience to His will.

Jesus Christ is the Lord of all of creation, the Lord of the universe. Paul wrote about Him in Ephesians, chapter one. He wrote of how "the God of our Lord Jesus Christ, the Father of glory . . . . with the working of the strength of His might which He brought about in Christ, when He raised Him from the dead, and seated Him at His right hand in the heavenly places, far above all rule and authority and power and dominion, and every name that is named, not only in this age, but also in the one to come. And He put all things in subjection under His feet, and gave Him as head over all things to the church, which is His body, the fulness of Him who fills all in all (Ephesians 1:17, 19–23). Paul also wrote in Philippians: ". . . God highly exalted Him, and bestowed on Him the name which is above every name, that at the name of Jesus every knee should bow, of those who are in heaven, and on earth, and under the earth, and that every tongue should confess that Jesus Christ is Lord, to the glory of God the Father" (Philippians 2:9–11).

The Holy Spirit is the Person who has been moving, or hovering, over the earth since the beginning (Genesis 1:2). He has been the One performing the works of God in the earth. As Moses led God's people out of Egypt, they were backed up against the Red Sea, with no apparent means of escape from Pharaoh's approaching soldiers. The Lord (I believe it was the Holy Spirit) spoke to Moses and told him to stretch his hand and staff out over the Red Sea and divide it (Exodus 14:15–16). In the parting of the Red Sea, the Holy Spirit caused a strong east wind (*rûach*) to separate the waters so that there was dry ground at least a half-mile wide, all the way across the Red Sea, so that the people could cross. This was a demonstration of power that could have been accomplished only by God.

God had put His Spirit upon Moses to lead His people. Then, as the burden became too great for Moses, God took of the Spirit who was upon Moses and put Him upon the seventy elders, so that they also would be empowered to serve (Numbers 11:17).

God's Spirit, the Holy Spirit, came upon Gideon to empower him for service (Judges 6:34), upon Samson (Judges 14:6), and upon Saul (I Samuel 10:10). In the Old Covenant, the Holy Spirit "came upon" certain people for certain tasks. The rest of the people of Israel had only their own limited human willpower to enable them to obey God. Individually, and as a people, they failed in spite of all the warnings that they were given through prophets whom God raised up to warn them. They were warned many times, but would soon be back into their sinful ways, with their backs turned to God. The eventual price of their failure was exile.

While they were in exile, Ezekiel was moved upon by the Holy Spirit to prophesy to God's people of a future time: "I will put My Spirit within you and cause you to walk in My statutes" (Ezekiel 36:27). So, at some time in the future, God's almighty Holy Spirit would come inside His people and empower them to be able to walk in obedience to Him (see Galatians 4:6). In the future, all of God's people would have the Holy Spirit within them, whereas in the Old Covenant, the Holy Spirit came upon only certain people. The Holy Spirit dwelling inside God's people would provide opportunity for a personal relationship with God.

Jesus taught His disciples about the coming Holy Spirit while He was with them here on earth. He said: "If any man is thirsty, let him come to Me and drink. He who believes in Me, as the Scripture said, 'From his innermost being shall flow rivers of living water.' But this He spoke of the Spirit, whom those who believed in Him were to receive; for the

Spirit was not yet given, because Jesus was not yet glorified" (John 7:37–39).

Much of John 14:15 through John 16:15 is devoted to Christ's teaching on the Holy Spirit. As part of that teaching, He explained that the Holy Spirit would convict men of their sin, that He would guide believers into all the truth, and that He would glorify Jesus. Jesus said, "He shall glorify Me; for He shall take of Mine, and shall disclose it to you. All things that the Father has are Mine; therefore I said, that He takes of Mine, and will disclose it to you" (John 16:14–15).

It is important to remember that one of the roles of the Holy Spirit is to glorify Jesus. When the Spirit does His amazing work here on the earth, it is entirely possible for people to not understand that it is the Spirit at work, and they want to give glory to the person through whom the Holy Spirit has worked. God does not want this. As Peter and John approached the "gate of the temple which is called Beautiful," the Holy Spirit led Peter to minister to the lame man at the gate, and he was miraculously healed, as described in Acts 3:1–8. On seeing this man healed in such a miraculous way, the people crowded around Peter and John, thinking that they were the source of the man's healing.

Then, the Holy Spirit prompted Peter: "But when Peter saw this, he replied to the people, 'Men of Israel, why do you marvel at this, or why do you gaze at us, as if by our own power or piety we had made him walk? . . . On the basis of faith in His name, it is the name of Jesus which has strengthened this man whom you see and know; and the faith which comes through Him has given him this perfect health in the presence of you all" (Acts 3:12, 16).

While it is important that we recognize the Holy Spirit as God and have great reverence and appreciation for Him, He wants us to give glory to Jesus, the Lord of the universe. Since Jesus ascended to the right hand of the Father, the Holy Spirit has been the primary Person of the Trinity who is active on the earth, God's "action Person." Jesus continues to reign over the universe from on high (Ephesians 1:18–23), as the Holy Spirit accomplishes His purposes here on earth, and in the lives of mankind, all to the glory of God.

The Holy Spirit's divine involvement in my life has been a great blessing. I will mention just one example. I had been the pastor of a small church in South Carolina for several years, when God called me to serve in a church in North Carolina. After I had been introduced to this church in North Carolina, and both their search committee and I had become convinced that this was the will of God, it was time for me to be examined by the ministerial committee of the presbytery in North Carolina. They would decide if they wanted to recommend me for approval to the whole presbytery at a meeting that was soon to occur.

During their examination, they concluded that they could not approve a pastor who believed in the current-day working of the gifts of the Holy Spirit and who was involved in such things. They voted to recommend that the presbytery turn me down. They told me to inform the chairman of the search committee of the North Carolina church that they would not give their approval and that I should withdraw my name from consideration. I called the chairman, and he told me that the search committee was convinced that God was calling me to their church, that they planned to present me to the whole presbytery, and to let them decide the issue, regardless of the examination committee's decision.

The afternoon before I was to be presented to the whole presbytery (approximately three hundred pastors and elders) with a negative recommendation, I was praying about it. I was telling God how I was dreading the unkind challenges I knew I would hear. I heard the Holy Spirit say to me, "If you will treat all of these pastors and elders with love and respect, I will flood you with my peace, and I will win the day." I was blessed by this but wasn't 100% sure that I had heard correctly.

After dinner that evening, I received a call from an elder in the North Carolina church; I had never met him personally. He said he had been praying for me and had been given a word from the Holy Spirit that he was to deliver to me. I asked him to give it to me. He said, "The Lord has said that if you will treat these pastors and elders with love and respect, He will flood you with His peace, and He will win the day." I wept with joy.

When I was presented at the meeting, the chairman of the examination committee said they had voted against me because they thought I was not suitable for this presbytery, and they were recommending that the presbytery vote the same way. Pastors and elders lined up at the microphone to challenge me with their questions. It was fierce. I responded with love and respect, and the Lord filled me with His peace. After about forty-five minutes of these fierce challenges, a pastor stood to speak in favor of my reception into the presbytery. Then I saw the Holy Spirit "turn the tide" of the meeting. Pastors and elders began to line up at the microphone in order to speak on my behalf. When the vote came, I was received into the presbytery by a unanimous vote. The chairman, who was very angry, voted against me, but the elder who was counting the votes did not see his hand raised.

The Holy Spirit is at work in the affairs of men. I am always encouraged by Proverbs 21:1: "The king's heart is like channels of water in the hand of the Lord; He turns it wherever He wishes." I have seen that if the Holy Spirit can turn the heart of the king, He can turn anyone's heart, since He is God. Over the years, I've seen the Holy Spirit move in the lives of hundreds of people, bringing them to deeper faith in Jesus as they trust Him to lead them by His Holy Spirit in various forms of ministry.

CHAPTER FOUR

His Personality

In this work, I have referred to the Holy Spirit as "He" or "Him," and not "It." This is a very important choice of words for every believer to make. If the Holy Spirit is an "it," and not a "He," but simply the power of God, then we can have no personal relationship with Him. Yet, Paul's benediction at the end of II Corinthians (13:14) speaks of fellowship with the Holy Spirit for believers. Paul lived in close fellowship with the Holy Spirit.

In Acts 13:2, Luke recorded that the Holy Spirit *said*, "Set apart for Me Barnabas and Saul for the work to which I have called them." Because the Spirit is a Person and He has us on His mind, He has things to say to us (see Acts 21:11 and I Timothy 4:1). The Holy Spirit spoke words that were clearly understood, and they were recorded. Only a Person can speak words.

In order for the Holy Spirit to be considered a Person, He must demonstrate that He has will, intelligence, and an ability to act, as in speaking. Scripture attests to these abilities: "Even so the thoughts of God no one knows except the Spirit of God" (I Corinthians 2:11). "But one and the same Spirit works all these things, distributing to each one individually just as He wills" (I Corinthians 12:11). He is our

Teacher (John 14:26). He is our Helper (John 14:16). He is our Sanctifier (John 17:17). He is our Guide (John 16:13). These activities require a personality.

Scripture also bears witness to the Holy Spirit being a Person by way of the personal pronouns used to reference Him. "When the Helper comes . . . He will bear witness of Me" (John 15:26). "I tell you the truth, it is to your advantage that I go away; for if I do not go away, the Helper shall not come to you; but if I go, I will send Him to you. And He, when He comes, will convict the world concerning sin . . ." (John 16:7–8). "When He, the Spirit of Truth, comes, He will guide you into all the truth; for He will not speak on His own initiative, but whatever He hears, He will speak; and He will disclose to you what is to come" (John 16:13; see also verses 14 and 15).

Because the Holy Spirit is a Person who has feelings, He has the same unfailing and unconditional love for us as do the Father and the Son. It is comforting to know that the Spirit has been sent to be with us and to live inside us, as Immanuel, God with us. Because He lives inside us, He knows our hearts fully. Because the Spirit is God, He knows exactly what is best for us. Out of His limitless wisdom and personal knowledge of each of us, He operates in our lives with that wisdom. Here is an example from my life.

When our 25th anniversary was approaching, I wanted to bless my wife with a Caribbean cruise. Carrie and I had never been on a cruise. Financially, it was going to be difficult to do this, and Carrie finally said she didn't want to go because she would have been uncomfortable during the whole cruise, knowing the financial consequences of such an expenditure.

When our 30th anniversary was approaching, we had the means to purchase tickets for the cruise, and I brought up the subject again. Carrie said, "Okay, but only if you promise me you will ask the Lord if this is okay with Him." I promised and then made the reservations for later in the year. I got busy and distracted for six months. Finally, Carrie asked if I had consulted the Lord. I confessed that I had not and went right into the den and entered into prayer.

Pretty quickly, I realized that I had actually been afraid that the Lord would say "no" because of all we could do for the Kingdom of God with that money. I knew that I had to ask Him, and so I began to picture the three-masted sailing ship that was in the short video that had been sent to us by the sponsors of the cruise.

Suddenly, in my mind, the Lord was showing me his own video of the ship. I saw a rectangular movie screen against a black background, and there was the ship floating on beautiful, tropical blue water, with all of its sails in place. It was so beautiful. I knew the Lord was getting ready to speak to me in one way or another. Suddenly, white capital letters appeared against the black background, under the movie screen, forming the word *COMPLIMENTS*. Concerning a planned cruise, I wondered what *COMPLIMENTS* could mean.

I asked, "Lord, what do you mean, *compliments?*" Then, just as suddenly, the word *MY* appeared before the word *COMPLIMENTS*. With tears rolling down my cheeks, I realized He was officially giving me this cruise, with His compliments. He was going to be able to run His Kingdom without the money we would use on this cruise. I was filled up with His love. I had felt His love before, but never with such a powerful anointing of His presence. It came to me that this great and tender love that God has for me as His redeemed child is a normal part of His personality—a very important and central part of His personality.

Scripture teaches us literally that "God is love," as we see in I John 4:16, and so it should not be a surprise to us to find that He loves us with this love that is bigger and better than any love we have ever known. Some might say, "God's love is not like the kind of love I want," but that is because they have not experienced God's love coming through one of His people in the way God means for it to flow through His people.

God is the author of love, and He knows exactly how our hearts need to be loved. He is quite able to love us in the ways that will bless us most deeply. It seems important that every Christian should get this settled in his heart: God loves me. He cherishes me and wants close fellowship with me, so that His love for me can be felt in my life on a regular basis. Therefore, I need to learn to be vulnerable to His love, so that my heart can receive it fully (see Romans 5:5).

Over the years, I have observed that most non-Christians, as well as many Christians, believe that if they had a real, personal encounter with the Lord, they would find Him unhappy with them. They think that if they could see His face they would see a look of disapproval on it. The truth is that all the people I have met who have had real, personal encounters with the Lord, in which they either saw Him appearing to them in some way or heard Him speak into their spirits, have been deeply touched by His love. They have received a deep reassurance of His love for them and have come to believe that He actually cherishes them as His own precious children. In many cases, this has deepened their intimacy with Him.

CHAPTER FIVE

His Part in Regeneration

In the beginning, in the Garden of Eden, before Adam and Eve sinned, they were in perfect relationship with God and with each other. Without sin, they could perfectly and unconditionally love each other and God. They had the capacity to act with good and pure motives, as well as the ability to obediently do the will of God.

At the moment of their sin, they forfeited their perfection and their ability to love unconditionally; they "fell" from their perfect condition. They became selfish and prideful and began to operate with impure motives, doing things that were contrary to the will of God. This has been the condition of mankind since that time.

In Ephesians 4:17–19, we are instructed to "walk no longer just as the Gentiles also walk, in the futility of their mind, being darkened in their understanding, excluded from the life of God, because of the ignorance that is in them, because of the hardness of their heart; and they, having become callous, have given themselves over to sensuality, for the practice of every kind of impurity with greediness." Those who are not Christians live in spiritual and emotional darkness, unable to see the beauty of Jesus Christ and lacking any true desire to be like Him.

This desperate condition is also described in II Corinthians 4:3–4, 6: ". . . Even if our gospel is veiled, it is veiled to those who are perishing, in whose case the god of this world has blinded the minds of the unbelieving, that they might not see the light of the gospel of the glory of Christ, who is the image of God. . . . For God, who said, 'Light shall shine out of darkness,' is the One who has shone in our hearts to give the light of the knowledge of the glory of God in the face of Christ." The devil, who is the god of this world, has blinded every human mind since the Fall, except the mind of Jesus. We must be rescued from this blindness. God moved upon us by His Holy Spirit to remove the veil (see II Corinthians 3:16–18) and bring us into His marvelous light (see I Peter 2:9), so that we could see the glory of God in Jesus Christ.

Throughout the history of mankind, people have sensed or known of our Divine Creator. Romans 1:19–21 explains that God has revealed Himself to mankind through creation. However, mankind has a fallen, self-centered nature and has refused to acknowledge God as God and to worship Him.

Mankind is still blinded by "the veil." We refuse to acknowledge our fallen nature and enter into an appropriate "Creator to created" relationship, in which we live in dependence upon God's grace and seek to please Him as a child would seek to please a parent. Instead, mankind has tried to gain an arm's-length approval and acceptance from God through a code of behavior that we think would satisfy God. We have tried to earn God's approval through our deeds, in a way that doesn't involve full surrender to God. This way of trying to earn salvation is known as "works salvation" and is the kind of effort that is used by those who have never been touched by the Gospel and by those who do not want to surrender to God's Son, Jesus Christ, as Lord and Savior.

This works salvation will never get us into Heaven (see James 2:10). This is why we have instances of a person attending church for many years, trying to earn God's acceptance through his works and yet never becoming a Christian. The "veil" is still there, even while he attends church. This person wants to be accepted by God on *his* terms through the works that he thinks are suitable and deserving of God's approval; his refusal to surrender to God makes him an enemy of God (see Romans 5:10).

Many Christians testify about growing up in church and "never hearing the Gospel." However, it is unlikely that they actually did not *hear* the Gospel, but rather that when they heard the Gospel the veil was still in place and so they did not *understand* the Gospel. Only as God drew them to Himself and removed the veil could they see and understand the beauty of the Gospel (II Corinthians 4:6).

In the Body of Christ there are some who believe that mankind is capable of seeing the beauty of the Gospel and of Jesus Christ at all times. They believe that a person—once presented with the truths of the Gospel—is capable of making a legitimate and intelligent choice to accept what Jesus did on the cross and to be saved. He thus determines his own eternal destiny. This is called the Arminian theological position, which asserts that the Christian also can decide, on his own, to reject his salvation and thus lose his salvation and perish in hell forever.

The Reformed theological position holds that the unsaved man's mind has been severely darkened. His nature is sinful and fallen, the veil of unbelief prevents him from perceiving Truth, and he is incapable of choosing Christ, because he is fully given over to pride, selfish motives, and a refusal to surrender to the Lordship of Jesus Christ. In fact, he is an enemy of God (Romans 5:10).

In order to be saved, the Lord must draw him by the Holy Spirit, remove the veil, and bring the light of the Gospel into his understanding. Then, the Lord extends His marvelous grace and imparts the saving faith that the person needs, so that he can embrace Jesus as his Lord and Savior.

We see in Ephesians 2:8–9 that the faith which saves him is a gift of God: "For by grace you have been saved through faith; and that not of yourselves, it is the gift of God; not as a result of works, that no one should boast." This Reformed position is the one that I hold, which I believe God has revealed to me, primarily through my study of the Scriptures.

Scripture teaches us that God the Father is omnipresent but that He also is manifestly present on His throne in Heaven. Jesus is seated at His right hand (see Hebrews 10:11–13). The Son of God became incarnate in the Person of Jesus of Nazareth, as He ministered on this earth. After His sacrificial death and His resurrection, He ascended to the right hand of the Father. From that position, He rules the universe (Ephesians 1:20–23).

The Father and the Son are in Heaven, but God has not abandoned us. The Holy Spirit has been sent to the earth to dwell in believers. He always knows the will of the Father and the Son, which is His will as well. The Holy Spirit serves the Godhead as the "action Person" on the earth, carrying out the will of the Godhead, doing the work of the Godhead.

Jesus said, "No one can come to Me, unless the Father who sent Me draws him; and I will raise him up on the last day" (John 6:44). As the action Person of the Trinity, the Holy Spirit is at work throughout the world, drawing people to Jesus Christ.

In John 6:37, Jesus said, "All that the Father gives Me shall come to Me; and the one who comes to Me I will certainly not cast out." Jesus is quite certain that when the Holy Spirit carries out the will of the Father, drawing a person to Christ, then that individual *will* be drawn to Jesus and into God's Kingdom. Jesus will keep him there and not cast him out.

The Holy Spirit draws people to Jesus in many ways, ways that are individually designed for each person. Then the Holy Spirit removes the enemy's veil, and the light of the glory of God shines in his heart and mind. His heart becomes open and able to receive the work of the Lord. Now he is able to see the beauty of Jesus Christ, and he *wants* a relationship with Him.

Regeneration is the work of God. In Ephesians 2:8–9, Paul told us that it is "by grace [that] you have been saved through faith; and that not of yourselves, it is a gift of God; not as a result of works, that no one should boast." That saving faith is a gift of God, imparted by the Holy Spirit at just the right time, enabling a person to embrace Jesus Christ and place his trust in Him. If we had decided to have faith in Christ because of some study we had done, then our faith would be a "work of our own hands," and very likely we would boast.

In this work of God, the Holy Spirit enters the human spirit to live there for the rest of our lives and does the biggest miracle that is ever done. We are regenerated: brought to life spiritually by the Holy Spirit. We become part of "a chosen race, a royal priesthood, a holy nation, a people for God's own possession, that . . . [we] may proclaim the excellencies of Him who has called . . . [us] out of darkness into His marvelous light" (I Peter 2:9).

Paul was a zealous Jew who believed Christianity was dangerous and cultish in nature, and he took drastic measures to stamp it out. He even watched over the robes of fellow zealous Jews as they stoned Stephen (see Acts 7:58). God wanted Paul (he was called "Saul" before he was regenerated) and drew him to Jesus in a dramatic manner (see Acts 9:3–6).

The Lord had plans to use Paul in powerful ways as His instrument of truth, bringing many to Christ. Later, Paul gave testimony to the words that Jesus spoke to him on the road to Damascus, when Jesus saved him and called him to reach the Gentiles: "To whom I am sending you, to open their eyes so that they may turn from darkness to light and from the dominion of Satan to God . . ." (Acts 26:17–18). Paul later wrote to the Colossians about this transformation: "For he delivered us from the domain of darkness, and transferred us to the kingdom of His beloved Son" (Colossians 1:13).

At the moment of regeneration, a person is born again, or born of the Spirit (John 3:3, 6). When the Holy Spirit comes to dwell inside a person, the transfer from the domain or kingdom of darkness to God's marvelous Kingdom of light takes place in the spiritual, or unseen, realm (see II Corinthians 4:18). The spiritual light that emanates from the Holy Spirit, who now lives inside the new believer, begins to drive darkness from the believer's heart and mind and to replace that darkness with His marvelous light.

When I was serving as a pastor in the late 1980s, a man made an appointment to see me because he had heard that I had been in the business world for a number of years before becoming a pastor. This gentleman had inherited a Christmas tree farm from his uncle, and he was bewildered about how to run this business. He came to ask what he should do.

When I began to ask him about what he was hearing from God when he prayed about it, his responses indicated that he probably was not a Christian. After I had shared some Scripture with him, and the Holy Spirit lifted the veil from his eyes, he came to the realization that he was not a Christian. I offered to help him become a Christian, and he wanted to pray a prayer of salvation with me. The Holy Spirit was working on him powerfully, and I discerned that this was his time to enter the Kingdom of God. We prayed, and he surrendered his life to Jesus as Lord and Savior.

Not more than ten seconds after the prayer ended and I had said "amen," the Holy Spirit, now living inside him, moved him to become very hungry for the Word of God. He grabbed my open Bible out of my hand and began to read where I had been reading. He began saying things like "Wow! Look at that! I've never seen that before! I never knew this!"

The Holy Spirit was shining His light from this new believer's spirit into his mind, will, and emotions, enlightening this new child of God regarding the Word of God. The man had become spiritually alive. He was now born again.

God has created humans to have three parts: body, soul, and spirit (the human spirit). I Thessalonians 5:23 and Hebrews 4:12 indicate that spirit and soul are separate parts of a person. The human spirit appears to be the "innermost" part of the human, also referred to as the "heart" or the "inner man."

In Galatians 4:6, the Apostle Paul tells us, "God has sent forth the Spirit of His Son into our hearts . . . ." The heart needs to be brought fully to life, so that it can function as a person's spiritual center and as the place where the Holy Spirit dwells. See Diagram 1.

Diagram 1

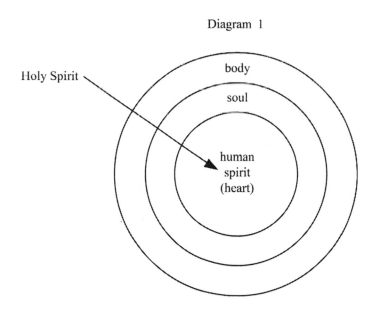

Diagram 1: The Holy Spirit enters man's spirit and brings it to life.

II Corinthians 5:17 says, "Therefore if any man is in Christ, he is a new creature; the old things passed away; behold, new things have come." However, we must acknowledge that when a person becomes a Christian all of his problems do not automatically go away. What does happen is that the Holy Spirit "rewires his operating system" so that He can use it, as He works supernaturally in and through believers.

As the Holy Spirit takes up residence inside the human spirit, He begins His work of conforming a believer "to the image of His |God's| Son" (Romans 8:29). This is the work of transforming the soul (the mind, will, and emotions), so that a believer becomes more and more Christlike and mature in the Spirit, over time. From within the human spirit, the Holy Spirit seeks to exert His influence out into the soul, so that He can conform the believer's mind, will, and emotions to the image of the Son.

In terms that may make this more easily understood, consider that He is shining His light out from our spirits into our souls, to minister healing and strength to the dark and broken places in our souls. See Diagram 2.

Diagram 2

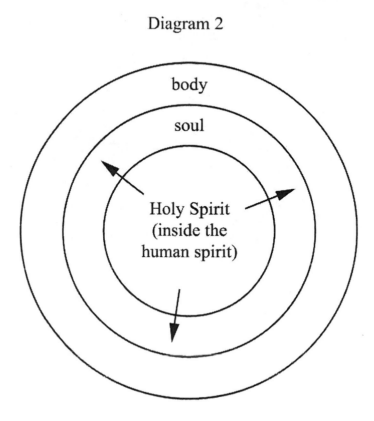

Diagram 2: The Holy Spirit at Work in the Christian

CHAPTER SIX

His Indwelling of the Believer

Under the unction of the Holy Spirit, the Apostle John recorded the following words of Jesus: "If any man is thirsty, let him come to Me and drink. He who believes in Me, as the Scripture said, 'From his innermost being shall flow rivers of living water' " (John 7:37–38). John then explained, "But this He spoke of the Spirit, whom those who believed in Him were to receive; for the Spirit was not yet given, because Jesus was not yet glorified" (John 7:39). John was inspired to write that believers were to receive the Holy Spirit. Centuries before, Ezekiel was inspired in the same way when he wrote these prophetic words: "I will put My Spirit within you and cause you to walk in My statutes" (Ezekiel 36:27). God had plans to begin to live inside His people by means of His Holy Spirit, at a time that He knew would be the right time.

After the New Testament church was born, Paul wrote to the Galatians: "When the fulness of the time came, God sent forth His Son, born of a woman, born under the Law, in order that He might redeem those who were under the Law, that we might receive the adoption as sons. And because you are sons, God has sent forth the Spirit of His Son into our hearts, crying, 'Abba! Father!' " (Galatians 4:4–6).

As we discussed earlier, the word *heart* (as the word is used here) does not mean the organ in the body that pumps blood. It means the innermost part, or the human spirit. This is where the Holy Spirit lives—in a person's spirit. From that central location, He wants to exert influence into the soul, which is made up of the mind, will, and emotions. All three of these areas need the ministry of the Holy Spirit.

At this place in our study, we need to make an important theological point. Any person who has trusted in Jesus Christ as his Savior and surrendered to Him as Lord of his life (see Romans 10:9) has received the Holy Spirit into his human spirit. In Romans 8:9 we read, ". . . If anyone does not have the Spirit of Christ, he does not belong to Him [God]." This makes it clear that if a person *does* have the Spirit of Christ, he *does* belong to God.

The most practical way to think about the difference between a Christian and a non-Christian is that the Christian has the Holy Spirit living inside of him and the non-Christian does not. It is the will of God that the lives of Christians should be noticeably different from those of non-Christians, because Christians have the Holy Spirit of God living in them. The surrender of our minds, wills, and emotions to the ministry of the Holy Spirit makes the difference in our lives.

Paul wrote to the Romans, ". . . Those who are in the flesh cannot please God. However you are not in the flesh but in the Spirit, if indeed the Spirit of God dwells in you" (Romans 8:8–9). Paul was showing us that it is the will of God for us to live our lives "in the Spirit." As we totally surrender to the control and empowering of the Holy Spirit, we can live according to the will of the Holy Spirit, according to the will of God. This is living in the Spirit. This should be a fervent goal of every Christian. Proverbs 3:6 tells us, "In all your ways acknowledge Him [God], and He will make your paths straight." A continuing awareness of His presence helps us follow the instruction of that verse. Living in the Spirit is one of the measures of Christian maturity. God is able to shine through us as we are in the Spirit. The only One who has ever done this perfectly is Jesus.

Paul had to reprimand the Corinthians for not living in the Spirit. He wrote: "I, brethren, could not speak to you as to spiritual men, but as to men of flesh, as to babes in Christ. . . . You are still fleshly. For since there is jealousy and strife among you, are you not fleshly, and are you not walking like mere men?" (I Corinthians 3:1–3). Paul believed he needed to remind them of the indwelling Holy Spirit: "Do you not know that you are a temple of God, and that the Spirit of God dwells in you?" (I Corinthians 3:16).

Paul shared with the Ephesians how he had prayed for them: "That He would grant you, according to the riches of His glory, to be strengthened with power through His Spirit in the inner man" (Ephesians 3:16). Here, Paul helps us see the importance of understanding that the Holy Spirit dwells in the inner man (the human spirit) and strengthens us.

Believers often think of God as being "out there" instead of being right here inside us. This helps explain why many believers do not seek an intimate relationship with God, the Holy Spirit. He wants this intimacy with us for the sake of every believer, as well as for the sake of the Body of Christ, so that we can glorify Him through our Spirit-filled lives.

In one of the churches I served, there was a woman in her mid-forties who was known as an intercessor and a devoted servant of God. I began to observe her ministry in the life of the church. I soon realized that she never spoke a negative word about anyone or anything, even though she was not shy about sharing her viewpoint. I saw goodness and gentleness and humility and love coming from her on an amazingly consistent basis. I realized that I was seeing the light of the Lord shining through her. She was walking as a child of light (see Ephesians 5:8), because the Holy Spirit was living in her.

I asked her how she managed that. She said that she had worked to cultivate a relationship with the Holy Spirit and that she had asked Him to enable her to relate to all people with love and forgiveness. She said that at first it took a lot of effort on her part to do what the Holy Spirit was showing her to do. As time passed, she learned to relax and let the Holy Spirit work through her. After a while, she noticed that the Holy Spirit so filled her heart with His love (see Romans 5:5) that she felt His empowering love flowing out of her to everyone. She said it blessed her immensely to be His vessel of love. She has a keen awareness of the Holy Spirit dwelling inside her. We would all do well to maintain such a keen awareness, consciously walking in close fellowship with Him.

CHAPTER SEVEN

His Part in Illumination and Guidance

J ust as a human father delights in the birth of his child and then in giving him illumination and guidance for his life, our Heavenly Father, even more so, delights in giving us new life in Christ (when we are born again) and then giving us the illumination and guidance we need for our lives and for our part in His Kingdom work. God wants His new children to learn how to receive the teaching of the Holy Spirit. John 14:26 says, "But the Helper, the Holy Spirit, whom the Father will send in My name, He will teach you all things, and bring to your remembrance all that I said to you."

Prior to receiving the Holy Spirit at the moment when we were born again, we could not receive what God had for us. It was foolishness to us, because we were "natural" men, men without the Holy Spirit. "A natural man does not accept the things of the Spirit of God; for they are foolishness to him, and he cannot understand them" (I Corinthians 2:14). We were blinded by the enemy, so that we could not see the light of the Gospel (II Corinthians 4:4). We needed supernatural illumination from the Holy Spirit. We give thanks to God because He "has shone in our hearts to give the light of the knowledge of the glory of God in the face of Christ" (II Corinthians 4:6).

Another important form of illumination that the Holy Spirit brings to us occurs during the renewing of our minds. As children, we accumulate information from the world around us, hundreds of thousands of information bits that are stored in our minds, as if on a computer's hard drive. While we are still children, we lack the maturity to discern between truth and error, and we accept as truth that which appeals to us. Because I watched Mighty Mouse cartoons as a child, I came to believe that the moon was made of cheese. It was a difficult day when I had to give up that notion a few years later. My mind was being renewed, as erroneous information was being replaced with accurate information.

The Lord wants to renew our minds. "Do not be conformed to this world, but be transformed by the renewing of your mind" (Romans 12:2). This work is done by the Holy Spirit in a mind that is surrendered to Him. It is a lifelong process. As the Holy Spirit begins to show us that we have been believing erroneous data and accepting it as truth, we become aware of our need to allow the Holy Spirit to do this transforming work in us.

The enemy has been diligently filling the world with subtle lies to ensnare God's people in ways that will hinder their faith and their ability to serve Him effectively (e.g., "I must be in control"). The Holy Spirit brings us His illumination to replace erroneous information. We are best served if we develop a hunger for this illumination, this exchange of truth for error. The primary source of God's truth is His Word, the Bible. We will practice good stewardship of our minds if we will regularly bathe our minds in the Word of God.

While we know that the Word of God is divinely inspired (II Timothy 3:16), we also know that in its written form it is of little value to a non-Christian, since he does not have the

Holy Spirit living inside him to illuminate the Scripture for his understanding. As the non-Christian is being drawn to the Lord, the Holy Spirit will illuminate particular parts of the Word that He plans to use as part of that person's salvation experience.

Once a person is born again, the Holy Spirit lives inside him, ready and eager to enable him to understand all of God's Word as he reads and studies it. Even among Christians, the Holy Spirit must be invited to provide understanding. Our spiritual posture is important here. If we are in a condition where we are spiritually closed down, because disturbing circumstances in our lives have caused us to temporarily turn away from God, not caring to hear from the Holy Spirit, we will get very little out of a teaching from the Word of God.

The Holy Spirit will not give up on a person who has turned away from Him. Just as He wooed the person to place his faith and trust in Jesus initially, He will call that person back to a place where he desires to receive from God. As the Holy Spirit brings the person closer to that place of desire, the person recalls his great need for the working of the Holy Spirit in his life.

In his first letter to the Corinthians, Paul referred to the need for the Holy Spirit to be moving in power while he preached in their midst, so that their "faith should not rest on the wisdom of men, but on the power of God" (I Corinthians 2:3–5). The Holy Spirit makes the Word of God, written or spoken, come alive for us in important ways, by the illumination He brings.

In today's modern church, all too many preachers believe that since the Scripture is now a completed work, it can be used like any other textbook can be used. Textbooks are often read and then forgotten, without making any lasting impact on the student. God wants a different result from the use of His Word. He said that as a result of proper sowing, watering, and tending, the earth will bear and sprout: ". . . So shall My word be which goes forth from My mouth; it shall not return to Me empty, without accomplishing what I desire . . ." (Isaiah 55:10–11).

When a preacher begins to prepare his message for Sunday morning, he can look at God's Word as a textbook and think about an efficient way to give a portion of this information to the people. If he prepares in this manner, the intended purpose of God's Word is not likely to be fulfilled. However, if a preacher sees the Word of God as God's very own words, living and breathing and supernaturally empowered by God to change and bless people, he will handle the Word differently than the other preacher handled it.

If the preacher asks God to anoint his mind and heart so he can hear what the Holy Spirit has to say to him as he studies during the preparation of his message, he will begin to have God's very words "cooking" in his heart. As he tends this "cooking pot" all week, God's message will come forth (sprout) into his understanding, and it will be ready on Sunday morning. The Holy Spirit gives illumination and guidance to preachers who ask for it and who then believe He will give it (James 1:6–8).

The Word of God will go forth "as from the mouth of God" when this same preacher is filled with the Holy Spirit, when he is so surrendered to the Holy Spirit (to His will, direction, and empowering) that he will even allow the Holy Spirit to change his message, right in the middle of preaching it. Such a surrendered instrument of God then becomes a fountain of the Word of God, empowered by the Holy Spirit, an instrument for God to use in the illumination of His people.

God wants us to understand His Word. He wants us to ask Him, "What does this verse mean, Lord?" He wants us to open up our minds and understanding to all of His Word as we study it. He does not want us to avoid verses we find difficult or those which seem to conflict with the theology we have been given.

As I mentioned in my introduction, I knew a pastor whose Sunday morning text was Matthew 3:1–12, and he just skipped right over verse 11 because he did not want to have to answer questions from his people about being baptized with the Holy Spirit. He had come to believe, through conversations with his peers, that this subject only brought controversy and division. Since the Lord led John the Baptist to say the words in verse 11, clearly, this is not His viewpoint. It is entirely possible that there are certain theological beliefs that we have accepted from others that are false. Through our years as Christians, God will periodically remind us, "Do not be conformed to this world, but be transformed by the renewing of your mind" (Romans 12:2).

God's Holy Spirit is "the Spirit of Truth" (John 16:13), and He wants to show us the truth, as He brings to us illumination about Himself, ourselves, and the world around us. Many people have held ideas and feelings about our Heavenly Father that are far different from those they held in regard to Jesus. An example of illumination that renews our minds is the occasion when Philip said, "Lord, show us the Father," and Jesus replied, "He who has seen Me has seen the Father" (John 14:8–9). That was very important illumination for Philip. There is more revelation that the Spirit of Truth wants to reveal to us as He guides us into all the truth. This illumination will come in various ways and will definitely be enhanced through the development of an intimate, personal relationship with Him.

As we live our lives and seek to serve our Lord, we need guidance. Our Heavenly Father very much wants to give that guidance to us. He gives it to us through the Holy Spirit, who lives right here inside us. Jesus declared Himself to be the Good Shepherd (John 10:11), and we believers are His sheep. As a sheep listens to the voice of its shepherd, so we are to listen to the Lord's voice. Jesus said that His sheep hear His voice (John 10:16, 27). He does not say that *some* of His sheep hear His voice, but that *all* of His sheep are able to hear His voice. This is a wonderful encouragement to us.

It is important to mention, however, that if we are expecting God's voice to sound like the voice of another human standing near us and speaking to us, then we may be disappointed or frustrated. Most Christians report hearing the voice of the Lord as an impression deep in their human spirit, and not like an audible voice. Once the impression is in a person's spirit, then the Holy Spirit imparts understanding to his soul (his mind, will, and emotions). This process generally happens rapidly.

Even then it is still possible not to feel certain that it is the Lord speaking. If we employ the concept God showed us concerning asking for wisdom, found in James 1:5–8, we find that we are admonished to "ask in faith without any doubting" (verse 6). This Scripture says that if someone doubts, he is a double-minded man, and a double-minded man will not receive anything from the Lord (verses 7–8).

For a Christian, double-mindedness on this subject suggests that a person's faith in God's love for him and God's desire to speak to him is not well developed. If a Christian is having trouble in this area, it is almost always helpful to go to God and confess that he is having trouble with his faith, confess that he doubts that God loves him enough to speak to him, confess that he doesn't feel worthy enough to have God speak to him, or tell God whatever may be bothering him. Then, he should ask the Lord to help him overcome this stumbling block, to reveal His love to him, and to give him confidence as he listens for the Lord's communication.

Those serving the Lord in the early church surely needed to hear the Lord's guidance. Peter and John were arrested and brought before the Jewish rulers, elders, and scribes. They were required to explain themselves (Acts 4:5–7). It is likely that Peter recalled the words of Jesus, when He said, "When they deliver you up, do not become anxious about how or what you will speak; for it shall be given you in that hour what you are to speak. For it is not you who speak, but it is the Spirit of your Father who speaks in you" (Matthew 10:19). Peter needed to hear from the Lord at that very moment. In Acts 4:8, we see that Peter began to speak what the Holy Spirit was giving him to speak.

While Saul, Barnabas, and other believers were gathered for prayer at Antioch, the Holy Spirit spoke into the spirit of one or more of those present with instructions to set Saul and Barnabas apart for a special work (Acts 13:1–3). It is highly likely that they talked about this among themselves and came to agreement that this was guidance from the Lord. Then, after laying hands on them and praying, they sent them on their way.

In Acts 16:6–7, we read about Paul, Silas, and Timothy hearing from the Holy Spirit that they were "forbidden by the Holy Spirit to speak the word in Asia." Sometimes the Holy Spirit says "no" to us, and this, too, is very important guidance.

The Holy Spirit is eager to give to us whatever we need, at just the right moment. Our part is to maintain an awareness of His presence in us and around us, as He is at work in the affairs of men. When we stay alert and attentive to His voice, we get to participate in what God is doing in the earth. He wants to use His children to minister to believers and non-believers. As we remain aware of His presence and available to Him for this purpose, we will be given many wonderful opportunities to bring blessing to many people, as the Lord works through us to accomplish His purposes.

As part of the illumination we need, the Holy Spirit also grants to us the gift of discerning of spirits (I Corinthians 12:10) as, and when, we need it. This means that we are enabled to know when a spirit other than the Holy Spirit is initiating something. Since the first century, the enemy has regularly been sending into the church wolves who appear as sheep; they are seeking to deceive and confuse God's sheep (see Acts 20:29–30). For example, an unsaved man may be guided by ungodly motives and intentions to become a controlling influence in a local church. God wants us to be able to discern this and take appropriate action against such "wolves." Sometimes, when they are exposed in the right way, they come under conviction and surrender their lives to Jesus. Sometimes the source of the problem is an evil spirit (demon). In that case, God provides the gift of discerning of spirits and wants the demon cast out (see Acts 16:16–18). Illumination is usually involved in the exercise of most of the nine gifts listed in I Corinthians 12:8–10.

The Holy Spirit's guidance in my life has been very important to me. Here is a significant example of His guidance in my life. Before I was ordained as a pastor, I worked in the business world. One of the areas of business I was involved in was real estate development. The year 1974 brought a recession in the United States, and it was very hard on real estate development. The small company I worked for went bankrupt. After several months of looking for a job, I discovered that real estate development companies had no interest in hiring anybody.

I decided to go back to school and get a master's degree in accounting, so that I could have a trade/talent that would always be in demand and so that I would be able to provide for my family. I was trusting in my own wisdom, at that point, out of my frustration in the job hunt. Just before I was to begin school, the Lord worked through someone I hardly knew to arrange for a real estate developer to offer me a job. He had a one-man operation, and he needed someone to come alongside him. The job had everything I wanted in my next job. It was "too good to be true." However, I was suspicious of this offer, as was my wife, because of what I had just been through in this recession. I wanted security for my family.

I went to a quiet place to pursue God's direction about this. I began to explain to God all about how this plan to equip myself with an accounting degree was the sound and smart thing to do and how I could bring security to my family through this pursuit. Soon, I sensed the Holy Spirit wanting me to be quiet and listen. Then the Holy Spirit said to me, "What is so secure about an accounting career?" As I sensed Him saying this to me, it seemed that He was smiling, as if to say, "You do remember, don't you?"

With resounding Holy Spirit-imparted clarity, I suddenly knew that no career created by man could ever be totally secure. I knew that only what God does can be secure. I knew that though I didn't know exactly where this job with this developer would lead, still *it was the will of God*. This wonderful Person, the Holy Spirit, knew exactly the way I needed to hear this admonition. He knew that it would press me back to the verse that I had chosen for my life verse: "Trust in the Lord with all your heart, and do not lean on your own understanding" (Proverbs 3:5).

As it turns out, the Lord used this job with the real estate developer as part of His means to call me to be a pastor. Within six months, the Holy Spirit had worked in the hearts of four employees for whom I was responsible to cause them to want me to minister God's Word to them on a weekly basis. As I taught them, the Holy Spirit was teaching me about being a pastor. I felt His personal love for me as I determined to follow His lead. About a year later, His undeniable calling to be a pastor was made clear to me, and I enrolled in seminary. Listening and following the Holy Spirit's guidance was very important to me.

CHAPTER EIGHT

His Part in Sanctification

From His place in the very center of every Christian, the Holy Spirit is at work carrying out God's plan for our personal sanctification. He is at work conforming us to the image of His Son (see Romans 8:29).

We are fully sanctified only upon our arrival in Heaven. When we are with the Lord in Heaven, we will be released from all the world's trappings and be made like Him for all eternity (Philippians 3:20–21). However, while we live on this earth, the Holy Spirit is at work doing as much of that work as we will permit Him to do.

He knows just which heart attitudes and behaviors need to be removed so that we can be salt and light to the world, so that the Lord's glory can be seen in us. The Holy Spirit wants to clear away the things that hinder the development of the fruit of the Spirit in our lives, so that His fruit can become evident. As we are empowered by His Holy Spirit, being freed up like this enables us to function more as the Lord intends for His children to function. This freedom also prepares us to yield to the Lord as He manifests the gifts of the Holy Spirit through us, for the benefit of those who need them.

This supernatural work of the Holy Spirit in our sanctification is a process that is taking place in every believer's life, but the ultimate result will be different in each life. God gives us the ability to choose how completely we will yield to and cooperate with His work of sanctification in our lives. Therefore, the amount of cooperation we offer has a significant effect on the outcome.

Many individuals are able to conduct their lives in very exemplary ways, reflect a caring attitude, be involved in the work of the church, and recite proper doctrine. However, some of these individuals have never experienced regeneration, and so they are not Christians. Their primary motivation is to be a part of a respectable group of people who serve in the community and care for each other, but they have no real interest in a personal relationship with Jesus. No sanctification has taken place in their lives since the Holy Spirit does not live in them. They have used their human willpower to conform to a system of behavior that they value, but their motives are still worldly, and they are seeking benefit, satisfaction, and approval for themselves through their association with Christians.

True sanctification brings about a supernatural and genuine change inside the individual, resulting in the release of God's supernatural love into that person's life (Romans 5:5) and consequently a desire to do God's will (Hebrews 13:20–21, Psalm 40:8). At the moment when God saves us, when we are born again, we enter the Kingdom of God with patterns of sin that were established earlier in our lives. It is God's plan to release us from the inner drive toward these sins. He wants to release us from hidden and known fears (see II Timothy 1:7) that lead us into patterns of avoidance, and He wants to release us from overt sinful practices. The Lord also wants to heal hurts or wounds that tend to keep us trapped in those fears and sinful practices, thus hindering our growth as Christians.

So, sanctification is not simply God teaching us how to live a more Christlike life. It also involves His supernatural healing of our lives in many different ways.

Here are two examples of our need for healing:

1. We are commanded to love God and to love our neighbor as ourselves (Matthew 22:37–39). Our neighbors are those people whom God puts into our lives. We will not be able to really love those neighbors with God's love if we have a fear of being vulnerable to others, since real love involves a certain measure of vulnerability. We need healing in order to get past the fear of being hurt if we allow ourselves to be vulnerable.

Furthermore, if we cooperate with God's plan of sanctification in our lives, yielding to the work of the Holy Spirit, then we will begin to identify unacceptable heart attitudes and behaviors that are not pleasing to God. This increasing ability to recognize these traits is part of God's sanctification process, as He shows us where changes need to be made.

2. God also wants us to manifest His peace in this stress-filled world. Our Lord Jesus said He wants us to have His peace (see John 14:27 and Philippians 4:6–7), but we cannot be filled with His peace if stress and anxiety are operating in our lives. We need to allow God to deliver us from stress. God is our Healer, and His Holy Spirit has important healing work to do in our emotions as part of His work of conforming us to the image of His Son.

Jesus told us, "You shall know the truth, and the truth shall make you free" (John 8:32). Will we decide to reject our old, ungodly beliefs and accept His truth and the changes it requires in our lives, so that we can be free? If our answer is yes, we need to ask Him to empower us to live in the reality of that truth, to believe it, and to make the changes that He wants to see in our lives, as we agree to work with Him in those changes.

Our faith in God's sanctifying work in our lives can be inspired by Proverbs 21:1: "The king's heart is like channels of water in the hand of the Lord; He turns it wherever He wishes." If He can change the heart of a king, He can change anyone's heart, even ours (see Daniel 4:28–37). The changes God will want to make are intended to conform us to the image of His Son.

When God begins His work of sanctification, we can expect to see the effects of it. We will see the beginning of the full development of the fruit of the Holy Spirit in us (see Galatians 5:22–23; also see the chapter on the fruit of the Holy Spirit).

Many men and women have had their lives changed significantly by the sanctifying work of the Holy Spirit. They have become people who love like they have never loved before, with a purity and caring that can come only from God. Where they had been rough and crude before, they have become gentle. Where they held deep grudges before, they have been enabled to forgive. Where they had been very selfish before, they have begun to serve the Lord and other people with their time and even with their money.

In the natural, this transformation is hard to comprehend. However, when we consider that the Holy Spirit of God lives inside them and is diligently at work in the process of conforming them to be like Jesus, we can understand that this supernatural work is simply our Heavenly Father at work by the Holy Spirit in the newly adopted children He loves.

The first thirty-two years of my life were lived outside the Kingdom of God and included growing up in a non-Christian home. As a result, I developed many worldly ways, including swearing. My school friends all swore with abandon. None of them was from a Christian home. My early adult years were lived in environments that were filled with swearing. I began to realize that the young women I dated did not appreciate my language, so I tried to cut back on the swearing. Then, as I was dating my future wife Carrie, it became clear that this habit would have to be nearly eliminated. So, in my own unregenerate strength, I tried to seriously curtail this long-held practice of swearing, with only a small amount of success.

During the first years of our marriage, efforts in my own strength brought only moderate success at curtailing the swearing. However, five years after we were married, the Lord saved me, and His Holy Spirit took up residence in me and began the process of sanctification in my life. I was so grateful for the forgiveness that was granted me and so eager to be God's man that I was open to whatever changes He wanted to make. As a result of my eager cooperation and His great power, the Lord was able to almost totally eradicate the practice of swearing within a month or so. Only occasionally did a swear word slip out, and now, many years later, only occasionally does one even come to mind. This amazed my wife and me. This could only be accomplished by the mighty power of God's Holy Spirit. "For this is the will of God, your sanctification" (I Thessalonians 4:3).

Each new believer enters the Kingdom of God with an assortment of worldly and ungodly ways in his life. Because God loves us so much, He is not willing to leave us in that condition. His sanctification process continues from the moment we are born again until we arrive in glory. Some of the things that need to be changed are hidden from our conscious minds. At just the right time, the Holy Spirit will bring them to our attention, with assurance that He will be doing the work of changing that behavior with our active cooperation. This work of God in us is nothing to dread or fear. It is a great blessing that He grants us because we are His children.

CHAPTER NINE

His Desire for Fellowship

God inspired Isaiah to prophecy that Immanuel (which means "God with us") would be born of a virgin girl (Isaiah 7:14). The idea of "God with us" has been in God's heart and mind from the beginning. When Jesus was born of the virgin girl named Mary, the prophecy was fulfilled, and the stage was set for His sacrificial death on the cross for us, for His resurrection, and for His ascension to the right hand of the Father, in Heaven. He knew that He would be leaving earth, but He would not leave us abandoned (John 14:18). God gave us His Holy Spirit, so that all Christians would have His Spirit living inside them.

It would not be possible for God to be any closer to us than this place where He lives inside us, in the Person of His Spirit. The Holy Spirit loves us, just as the Father and the Son love us. His love is unfailing, steady, strong, and very attentive. We are precious to Him. He pays attention to everything we do. He listens to our breathing as we sleep. He wants to have daily fellowship with us. The Apostle Paul enjoyed close fellowship with the Holy Spirit and heard from Him regularly. Paul wanted us to enjoy this same close fellowship with the Spirit. Paul ended his second letter to the Corinthians with these words: "The grace of the Lord Jesus

Christ, and the love of God, and the fellowship of the Holy Spirit, be with you all" (II Corinthians 13:14).

The book of Acts describes the early growth of the Christian church. It was not without personal cost to Christians, who were persecuted, often beaten, deprived of opportunity, ruined financially, and killed. They desperately needed the fellowship of the Holy Spirit. In the midst of their sufferings, they pursued and enjoyed this fellowship, and "the church throughout all Judea and Galilee and Samaria enjoyed peace, being built up; and, going on in the fear of the Lord and in the comfort of the Holy Spirit, it continued to increase" (Acts 9:31). The Holy Spirit comforted them during their trials. He strengthened them in their faith as they grew to know Him. This first generation of Christians had forsaken self-sufficiency and yielded full control of their lives to God. Now, they had to depend on Him.

In Proverbs 3:5–6 we are instructed, "Trust in the Lord with all your heart, and do not lean on your own understanding. In all your ways acknowledge Him, and He will make your paths straight." God wants us to trust Him, no matter what our circumstances cause our minds to think or "understand." Our wisdom is so inferior to God's wisdom. He wants us to acknowledge Him every day, at the beginning of the day. Speak to him. Greet Him with something like "Good morning, Lord." If we take some time to wait for His response, we will sense His love for us and His presence with us as we have fellowship together.

When we are "acknowledging Him in all our ways," we have our minds and hearts open to Him throughout the day, so that He can show us things, guide us, and speak to us. He wants us to be "people of the Holy Spirit." Non-Christians may think we are different, even strange, but they will often ask us to pray for them. They often believe that we "have connections upstairs." Often, they are jealous of our relationship with God. Paul pointed out that salvation came to the

Gentiles to make the Jews jealous (Romans 11:11). As we fellowship with the Holy Spirit, we come to love Him, and He does a deep work in us, conforming us to the image of the Son. His fruit in our lives begins to mature (see Galatians 5:22–23), and this makes us more attractive in the eyes of our neighbors.

As we grow in the grace and knowledge of our Savior, our neighbors are more and more attracted to our Lord as they see Him through us. Perhaps a time comes when my non-Christian neighbor wants to know about my relationship with God. He doesn't understand it, and he is curious. Such an inquiry is often the beginning of an opportunity that God is preparing, in which we have a chance to tell someone about our Savior, the Lord Jesus Christ. What a privilege it is to be able to lead others into the Lord's Kingdom!

One of the Holy Spirit's perpetual functions in our lives is to continually reassure us that we are saved. He "bears witness with our spirit that we are children of God" (Romans 8:16). He does not do that with non-Christians, since He does not live inside them. They may have gone to church all of their lives and may even sing in the choir, but they have no confidence that they will go to Heaven when they die.

In our flesh, almost all of us have a tendency to be independent and self-sufficient; we do not like to have to depend on anyone. Therefore, if we do not have close fellowship with the Holy Spirit, we try to live the Christian life in our own strength, through our own "good works." We form our own opinions about the things *we* think a person *must do* in order to be considered a Christian. We may become critical of others. We move away from our dependence on the grace of God.

When we were born again, we recognized that we had been rescued out of darkness and were brought into God's marvelous light by the work of the Holy Spirit. We knew we did not deserve this. We were sinners, and enemies of

God (Romans 5:10), yet He saved us by extending to us His wonderful grace, His undeserved favor. He opened our eyes with His marvelous light and gave us the faith to see the excellence of His Son, Jesus (Ephesians 2:8–9). With this faith, we embraced Jesus as Savior and surrendered to Him as Lord. In that moment, we entered His Kingdom and the Holy Spirit took up residence inside us. We were very grateful.

Now, do we think we have to keep ourselves saved by our good works? This would require us, in our own wisdom and strength, to live in perfect obedience to God, which we are unable to do. Paul had to correct the Galatians on this point: "Are you so foolish? Having begun by the Spirit, are you now being perfected by the flesh [your own works]? Does He then, who provides you with the Spirit and works miracles among you, do it by works of the Law, or by hearing with faith?" (Galatians 3:3, 5).

The Lord wants us to continue to trust in His original decision to extend grace and to give saving faith to us. He did not do this as an experiment, to see how we would do with His salvation. This was a permanent arrangement (see I Peter 1:3–5, Jude 1:1). When we allow the Holy Spirit to give us that continuing assurance of our salvation, we do not have to worry about not being perfect. Of course, out of our genuine love for Jesus and gratitude toward Him, we will try to live holy lives, to honor Him. However, if He had expected us to be perfect, He would not have spoken such strong words of correction about our idea that we have no sin. He would not have provided the way for us always to be able to receive forgiveness for sin, as recorded in I John 1:8–9. When the Greek word *teleios* is used in the New Testament, as in "you are to be perfect [*teleios*] as your heavenly Father is perfect" (Matthew 5:48), it means "filled, complete, or mature." It does not mean perfect in the sense of being without flaw. He knows we will have flaws until we are in Heaven.

Now that we are in His Kingdom, declared to be His children, we are free to walk in fellowship with the Holy Spirit, openly seeking more sanctification, more maturity in the Spirit, and also asking Him about what things He would have us do to serve Him. What a joy and a privilege it is to have fellowship with the Holy Spirit. He loves us just as Jesus loves us and desires to spend time with us in fellowship. He is right there when we take the time to be with Him and talk with Him, sharing our hearts with Him and seeking to learn what is in His heart.

My oldest daughter, Laura, became a Christian when she was six years old. A few years later, when she was nine, we were living in a different town while I attended seminary. As an outsider, getting to know new girlfriends was not easy. Then a girl in school invited Laura to spend the afternoon with her, after school. When Laura was dropped off at this girl's home, she found that another girl had been invited also. This didn't work very well. Later, on the way home with her mother, Laura cried with disappointment.

From Laura's perspective, the hostess girl had been "mean." Laura did not perceive that she had been at all responsible for any of the problems that afternoon. Her mother asked her to ask God to show her what part she had played in the problems. After some hesitations over whether she had any part in the conflict and whether she would even be able to receive anything from God, Laura went to her room to pray and ask God. Since girls can remember every word of every conversation they ever have, she went over every word of the conversation that had occurred among the three of them during the afternoon.

To Laura's total amazement, as she remembered what was said she saw it written above the head of the one speaking, in a bubble, just like in the funny pages of the newspaper. An even greater surprise was that on bubbles that contained words which had contributed to the conflicts that afternoon, the Lord colored the outlines of the bubbles red! Several of the red-colored bubbles contained *her* words, and then she saw that she surely *had* contributed to the problem. She came from her room amazed and excited that the Holy Spirit had shown her the truth. She was able to forgive the other girls. The Holy Spirit delighted in being with her during that time and helping her with her struggle. He showed her that He is right there, listening to everything she says to Him and seeking fellowship with her.

Because the Holy Spirit lives in us He is always with us, but he reveals Himself in different ways, at different times, with different people. A friend of mine went on a retreat into the mountains of Colorado with some other men. They went for Christian fellowship with one another, but they also purposed to seek God there. My friend was excited about having an encounter with God and was fairly certain this would happen, even though he was not very experienced at this. He wanted God to "show up" in some way that was obvious to him.

One day the men went climbing up the rocky slopes in different directions to have time alone with God. My friend climbed up a fairly steep cliff, and part of the way up he paused and spotted a bird on a branch of a tall pine tree that was growing up right alongside the cliff, not more than twenty feet from the cliff. This bird was watching him intently. As he looked at the bird looking at him, he thought, "God is looking at me right now. I just know it." He could sort of feel God's presence. He resumed his climb, and about ten minutes later, he was sitting on top of the cliff, looking out at a wonderful view. He glanced over to his right, and that same bird was sitting about ten feet from him looking out at the same view and then over at him. He suddenly felt the Holy Spirit's presence enfolding him in love, and he wept openly. He knew better than to believe that the bird was God, but he was pretty sure the Holy Spirit had sent the bird.

He became aware that the Holy Spirit was very pleased to be with him while he climbed in the mountains of Colorado and also was pleased to manifest Himself to my friend in response to his yearning for God's presence.

This friend is learning to pay attention to the presence of the Holy Spirit inside him and to listen for communication from the Holy Spirit when he feels a need for direction, encouragement, or even understanding of a situation. He finds fellowship with the Holy Spirit to be a very precious part of his Christian life.

CHAPTER TEN

His Fruit

One of the ways God manifests Himself in the lives of His children is through the fruit of the Holy Spirit. These fruit are literally part of the manifestation of the ministry of the Holy Spirit.

When we consider how the Greek word *karpos* (fruit) is used in the New Testament, we discover that it is used in four primary ways. The word *fruit* is used to literally describe the fruit that grows on a tree, "every good tree bears good fruit" (Matthew 7:17). *Karpos* is used to describe a Christian bringing forth the fruit of godliness in word and deed into his worldly surroundings (Colossians 1:10). It is used to describe a kind of spiritual holiness, "the fruit of the light consists in all goodness and righteousness and truth" (Ephesians 5:9). Then, *karpos* is used in the phrase "fruit of the Spirit." It is this last usage that we want to examine more closely.

The nine fruit of the Spirit listed in Galatians 5:22–23 are presented to us in striking contrast to the "deeds of the flesh," some of which are listed in verses 19 through 21.

The Fruit of the Spirit

·Love	·Patience	·Faith
·Joy	·Kindness	·Gentleness
·Peace	·Goodness	·Self-control

Some scholars have taken the position that since the list of the deeds of the flesh seems not to be an exhaustive list, then the list of the nine fruit of the Spirit also must not be exhaustive. While this is a possibility, we can realize that a person in whom all of the fruit are fully matured will live and behave very much like Jesus. To have this list of the fruit of the Holy Spirit developed to maturity in one's life is a grand, lifelong goal. Therefore, though I don't rule out the possibility, it doesn't seem likely that there are mentions of numerous other fruit sprinkled throughout the New Testament.

Another significant way that God manifests Himself in the lives of His children through the Holy Spirit is through giving the gifts of the Holy Spirit. There is a significant difference between the way the gifts and the fruit operate in our lives. The gifts are just that—they are gifts. We do not deserve to have them operate in our lives. We have not done anything to earn this privilege. We cannot make the gifts better or worse. They are from the Holy Spirit. They are used primarily in times of ministry. Their manifestation is never a result of our initiation. We should learn how to recognize when the Spirit wants to use His gifts through us, and we should learn how to cooperate with their proper operation. The gifts of the Spirit will be discussed in the next chapter.

On the other hand, we play a comparatively large part in the development of the fruit of the Spirit in our lives. As the fruit are developed, they are manifested in our behavior, as part of our personality. The fruit are from the Holy Spirit, but He wants us to voluntarily and purposely pursue their maturity in our lives. Most Christians want more love, joy, peace, etc., in their lives but have given this idea of the development of the fruit of the Holy Spirit very little thought. Therefore, they have not done much work on their development, if any. Some have even taken this position: "If God wants these fruit developed in me, He will have to do it, since I do not understand this very well."

As a result of this lack of understanding and initiative on the part of most Christians, the fruit of the Spirit are quite underdeveloped in their lives. The Lord wants each of the nine kinds of fruit fully developed "on our tree," like fully ripened peaches, with a sweet aroma. Unfortunately, most Christians' fruit look like "hard little green things" on the branches of their trees, because their "fruit trees" have not been tended or cultivated. Let us consider some of these fruit and what may be hindering their development.

When we consider love, the first fruit on the list, we must recognize that this is *agape* love, the love that is from God. He has told us in Romans 5:5, ". . . The love of God has been poured out within our hearts through the Holy Spirit who was given to us." The Holy Spirit has an endless supply of *agape* love, which He is happy to supply to our hearts, so that from our hearts we can manifest His love to everyone: our neighbors and those who persecute us, as well as to those who love us.

Many Christians are not loving others as the Lord wants them to love others, because they are afraid of the vulnerability that must be involved in loving a person and because of the fear of rejection. The fruit of love is still a "hard little green thing" on their trees. These Christians need healing in their souls, which will release them from their fears. Most of them need a deeper understanding of God's love for them.

In I John 4:18 we see that His perfect love drives out fear. Fearful believers need to let God's love fill them and drive out the fear. However, as odd as it may seem, many of them are afraid to let God love them—and they don't even know it. They don't have a correct understanding of how He loves them so passionately and yet so tenderly. They have a fear that His love is likely to mean that they will be specially chosen to become martyrs for the Kingdom or that they will be called upon to suffer in some way for God. This is not an accurate picture of God's love. When a Christian gets past his fear of vulnerability and speaks lovingly to a cashier at the market, for example, he is likely to find that the cashier responds in some loving way. This is Christian living.

I was one of those who needed the Lord to do a work in me to enable me to move into the level of vulnerability necessary for His love to flow out from me. Over the years, I have consciously worked on this. It all paid off when I was asked to visit a man in the hospital who was dying of lung cancer. I did not know him, but his daughter, who was a Christian, had called me from a distant city and told me that her father was not saved and that she was really worried about his eternal destiny. He had been kind of a ruthless businessman and not a good father or husband.

Tony was sixty-two. I was sixty-two. Before I went into his room and introduced myself to him, I prayed for God to fill me with His love for Tony. God was at work in our conversation of about ten minutes, when suddenly I felt this amazing welling up of God's love for Tony. My eyes were becoming moist as I felt this emotion. Finally, I said, "Tony, I hope you are alright with this. Suddenly, I'm feeling God's love for you in my heart. I just love you, Tony. Is that alright with you?"

He said, "Well, it's kinda weird, but I like it."

I said, "Good, because it's for real."

I left shortly after that. I met with him two more times, and on the last time the Lord drew upon the "bank account of love" I had established, and I was able to lead him into a saving relationship with Jesus Christ. He died two days later.

His unsaved widow asked me to preach his funeral, and I was able to present the Gospel in a very loving manner to all his unsaved friends.

The second fruit of the Spirit is joy. The Lord wants us to be filled with joy, yet a great many Christians believe that to be joy-filled is frivolous, or they believe that being joy-filled would make them too vulnerable to disappointment. However, Jesus said to His disciples, "These things I have spoken to you, that My joy may be in you, and that your joy may be made full" (John 15:11, see also Psalm 16:11, Nehemiah 8:10). Many others cannot allow the joy of the Holy Spirit to work in their lives because of emotional pain, unforgiveness, and other factors. If they will receive ministry for the healing of their wounded souls, they will find that the Holy Spirit will begin to build joy in their hearts. Paul wrote that "the kingdom of God is not eating and drinking, but righteousness and peace and joy in the Holy Spirit" (Romans 14:17).

The third fruit, peace, is essential to enable Christians to live "in the Spirit" (Romans 8:6). All too many Christians have had experiences of the peace that Jesus offers but have had that peace stolen away from them by worry, anxiety, and stress. Jesus has told us, "Peace I leave with you; My peace I give to you; not as the world gives, do I give to you. Let not your heart be troubled, not let it be fearful" (John 14:27). Through the Holy Spirit, Jesus is supplying the peace that we need, but we have not learned how to keep and protect that peace in our hearts. Christians have not learned to trust Him to be there for them, day in and day out. Instead, they continue to trust in themselves rather than trusting the Lord, even though there is an inner awareness that they cannot be "the Sovereign One" for themselves. This leaves them with stress instead of peace (see Philippians 4:6–7, I Peter 5:7). The more deeply surrendered to God they become, the more the peace of the Holy Spirit will reside within them. God's peace, which sustains believers in the midst of the difficulties of life, is a strong aroma that draws non-believers to Christ.

Next in the list is patience. Christians sometimes make a joke: "Do not ever ask God to give you more patience. He will put you through something that will really test your patience." This is the thinking of a person who is trying to work patience in his life through his own efforts, without letting the Holy Spirit provide *His* patience, the fruit of patience. A lack of patience is exposed most often when we become impatient with people, and we become impatient with people largely because we have unrealistic expectations of them. One might say, "But the Bible says he is supposed to do this!" We need to ask ourselves, "Is he really capable of doing this, at this point in time? Does he need to learn more about how to do this?"

We need to ask God to give us realistic expectations of others. If we have realistic expectations, then we will not be so disappointed with others' behavior. As we recognize shortcomings and failures in their lives, we can intercede for them, asking God to bless them and help them develop in the ways that they should, as they grow toward Christian maturity.

The fruits of kindness and goodness are similar. However, as you are working on each of them, asking God to bring His revelation to you about them, you will discover His explanation of the difference between the two. As we work on both of these, the worldly teaching that we are supposed to honor ourselves as Number One has to be defeated. The driving, "take no prisoners" kind of business leader will have to rethink his entire approach to life.

Jesus' teaching in Matthew 20:25–28 is helpful. In verse 28, Jesus said, "The Son of Man did not come to be served, but to serve, and to give His life a ransom for many." While He walked on the earth with His disciples, Jesus was a servant leader, always seeking ways to bless His disciples. As we seek ways to bless others, we will develop the fruits of kindness and goodness. In this world, these fruits are not plentiful, and the manifestation of them in our lives is a glorious witness of the presence of God's Spirit living in us.

Many of our Bibles list faithfulness as the next fruit. Explanation is made in commentaries that the words *kindness, goodness*, and *gentleness* surround this word, and it is supposed that Paul meant to include faithfulness as another human trait that blesses relationships in the Body of Christ. However, the Greek word *pistis* is used at this place in the original Greek text of the New Testament. This Greek word is normally translated as *faith*. The Authorized Version uses the word *faith*. A thorough study can be made in Bauer's *Greek-English Lexicon of the New Testament*, pages 668–670.

As I have considered this issue, I have come to believe the Lord wants us to remember that faith is given to us by the Holy Spirit. Anything that we might create and call faith certainly will not stand the tests of life that the Lord knows we will face. He gave us the faith we needed for salvation (see Ephesians 2:8). He gives us a special "gift of faith" for that extraordinary occasion when He will ask us to do something for Him that requires faith way beyond the faith that we have at that moment (see I Corinthians 12:9). Meanwhile, we live with a daily faith that is in between those two kinds. This is the fruit of faith supplied by the Holy Spirit, which is supposed to be cultivated and grown into stronger and stronger faith as we mature as Christians. It is like a muscle. If we exercise it regularly, it will grow and become strong. If we neglect it, it will remain small and probably not be of much use when we need to have strong faith during difficult times in the future.

So, we have three kinds of faith:

Saving Faith: given by the Holy Spirit for that glorious moment when we are born again (Ephesians 2:8).

Fruit of Faith: continually supplied by the Holy Spirit, but growing in size as we use it (Galatians 5:22).

Gift of Faith: given by the Holy Spirit for that extraordinary time when we need "faith to move a mountain" (I Corinthians 12:9).

The fruit of gentleness develops as we begin to truly care about the well-being of others. We read in Ephesians 4:15 that we are to "speak the truth in love." For some Christians, the invitation to speak the truth seems to sanction an opportunity to hurl accusations, which are often harmful. To speak the truth in love requires the fruit of gentleness, which will guide the speaker to make sure the person feels loved even after receiving the truth. True gentleness will bless others and will almost always avoid offending others.

The fruit of self-control can be misunderstood. It is not the will of God for us to try to be totally in control of our lives, which would reflect the belief that we do not need God. It is the will of God that He be in control as the Holy Spirit guides and empowers us. We do have the freedom to choose wrong and foolish behavior, even if the Holy Spirit is leading us to choose Godly ways. We have a choice. The fruit of self-control is the Holy Spirit enabling us to choose His ways. So, our fruit of self-control enables us to choose to be led by the Holy Spirit to live in His Godly ways, rather than allowing our flesh to direct our lives.

Our own personal process of sanctification, which includes the healing of our hearts, will be greatly helped if we purpose to work on the development of each fruit of the Spirit. It would probably be helpful for you to write the name of each fruit on a separate 3 x 5 card. Then, on that card, write the Scriptures which you can find that are helpful in the development of that particular fruit. Work on the development of that fruit for a week, praying about it each morning. It would be good to ask God to reveal anything in your life that may be hindering the growth of that fruit.

If we work on each fruit for a week, we will develop a little "workshop" for each fruit, so that we can work on them for the rest of our lives as we seek to be conformed to the image of Jesus Christ. God is able to provide all that we need in order to grow the fruit of the Holy Spirit into fragrant, mature fruit that will glorify Him and bless lives, including our own lives. The Holy Spirit will help us, if we will ask Him for that help.

CHAPTER ELEVEN

His Gifts

The ministry of Jesus here on the earth was filled with the love of God for people, as He announced that the Kingdom of God was at hand. It was also accompanied by mighty works of God: signs and wonders, miracles, healings, and casting out of demons. These works were a manifestation of God's love for people and an important part of God's preparation of their hearts to accept salvation. They were also a powerful encouragement to those who had already placed their trust in Him, in the sense that the works confirmed that they were trusting in a supernatural and loving God who was willing to use His power on their behalf.

When Philip requested that Jesus show them the Father, Jesus said, "Do you not believe that I am in the Father, and the Father is in Me? The words that I say to you I do not speak on My own initiative, but the Father abiding in Me does His works. Believe Me that I am in the Father, and the Father in Me; otherwise believe on account of the works themselves" (John 14:10–11). Jesus did not hesitate to point to the miraculous as a true sign that God was working among them. He knew that the Father intended for these signs to have a powerful effect on people. In addition, Jesus knew that it was the Father's will to continue to work miraculously here on earth as long as there is an earth.

The Jewish leaders were very concerned about this. John wrote, "Therefore the chief priests and the Pharisees convened a council, and were saying, 'What are we doing? For this man is performing many signs. If we let Him go on like this, all men will believe in Him, and the Romans will come and take away both our place and our nation' " (John 11:47–48).

Jesus explained that these works, or signs, were appropriate and made manifest by the Father for the healing and blessing of people, as well as a means of building faith in the hearts of the people. Jesus also explained to His disciples that this very ministry would be theirs: "Truly, truly, I say to you, he who believes in Me, the works that I do shall he do also; and greater works than these shall he do; because I go to the Father" (John 14:12). In the modern church today, there is widespread lack of understanding that the miraculous works Jesus said we would accomplish for Him would be done through *us* by His Holy Spirit.

Many modern Christians have said, "Yes, we can see that He said, 'He who believes in me would do His works,' and that this includes us, not just the first-century apostles, but how can we possibly do these miracles of Jesus?" Since these Christians do not believe they can do these things, they take the position that these things do not happen any more. Without realizing it, they have challenged Jesus' very words, found in John 14:12. Jesus knew that the Holy Spirit would be using His gifts to conduct His supernatural ministry here on the earth, using faithful Christians, throughout time. Today, we can see that in those places on the earth where signs and wonders are happening, people are coming to Christ in great numbers. Where there are no signs and wonders, evangelism is not nearly as effective.

There are several kinds of gifts mentioned in the New Testament. There is a category of gifts that are described by the Greek words *doron, dorea,* and *doma.* These kinds of gifts are similar to what we would call a "present."

The Greek word *charisma* means "grace-gift" or "gift of grace." It includes the Greek word *charis,* which means "grace." We will focus on this form of gift, since it reveals that God has graced us beyond what we deserve.

Gifts from God have been given by each Person of the Trinity:

God the Father has given us what are usually called the *motivational gifts.* These are listed in Romans 12:6–8. They are:

- Prophecy
- Exhortation
- Mercy
- Service
- Giving
- Teaching
- Leadership

The motivational gift of prophecy is different than the manifestational gift of prophecy (more information about the manifestational gifts will be given later in this chapter). A person with the motivational gift of prophecy is often described as being "prophecy-motivated." This means that he or she "sees things as black or white," without much "gray area," as a prophet would tend to view things. This person has a keen eye for what is right or wrong and does not mind saying so. This person usually has exceptional discernment.

It appears that these motivational gifts are the ones referred to by Peter when he said, in I Peter 4:10, that each has received a "special gift." These gifts seem to be supernaturally placed by God into each of us, providing a kind of central motivation in our lives. A person with the gift of mercy, for example, will be known by his or her friends as a merciful person. For further study on the motivational gifts, I recommend that you read Don and Katie Fortune's book titled *Discover Your God-Given Gifts*.

Jesus also has given gifts to the Body of Christ. We read in Ephesians 4:7–11 that He bestowed upon the Body the gifts of:

- Apostles
- Prophets
- Evangelists
- Pastors
- Teachers

These *ministry gifts* from Jesus to the Body of Christ are individuals who have been called by God to serve Him in these five different roles. It is the will of God that the Body of Christ recognize those who have been called to these roles by the Lord.

The Holy Spirit also has given gifts to the Body of Christ. The gifts of the Spirit that are listed in I Corinthians 12:8–10 are gifts of grace, given by the Holy Spirit to individuals and groups to meet their needs at the moment that they need them. Christians who are willingly available to God are used to deliver these gifts to those who need them.

These gifts are frequently called the *manifestational gifts*, because we read in I Corinthians 12:7 that "each one is given the manifestation of the Spirit for the common good." This means that each Christian has the Holy Spirit living inside of him, and therefore he is a vessel for the Lord to use. Each of us can be used by the Lord as a vessel for delivery of a gift of the Holy Spirit as He manifests Himself to the one who needs the gift.

The manifestational gifts are:

• Word of wisdom
• Word of knowledge
• Faith
• Gifts of healings
• Miracles
• Prophecy
• Discerning of spirits
• Tongues
• Interpretation of tongues

To illustrate how these gifts operate, we will speak for a moment about "gifts of healings." There is a great need for healing throughout the world. However, there are not many Christians who are willing to do what is necessary to be one of God's instruments to deliver a gift of healing. Christians fear being rejected by skeptics for merely being involved in this kind of ministry. Some Christians fear that they will pray for someone and that person won't be healed. These Christians have forgotten that it is God who heals, and it is up to Him to do the healing, not us. When I'm asked to pray, I will sometimes say, "Well, let's pray and see what God does."

God uses as His instruments people who are *willing* to be used, so that His gifts can be delivered to those who need them, for their benefit and blessing. Those individuals who are willing to be used have to be willing also to deal with the criticism and suspicion that often come as a result of involvement with supernatural ministry. When involved with supernatural ministry, Christians have to successfully fight against the temptation to be prideful. Some have to deal with their own fear of failure, since ministry to a certain person may appear to be unsuccessful. This has to remain

God's ministry, by His Holy Spirit. We are just the instruments, like a messenger who delivers a letter to someone.

When a particular person is used frequently by God to deliver gifts of healings to sick people, we can say that "God is using that person in the ministry of healing." It is not accurate to say that person "has the gift of healing." The gift belongs to the Holy Spirit and He gives the gifts when He sees that it is appropriate. As God's children, we are to remain available and "tuned in" to the Holy Spirit, so that He can prompt us to deliver a gift when He is ready. The next step is to be His obedient servant.

In I Corinthians 12:4, we see that there are varieties of *gifts*, but the same Spirit (the gifts are from the Holy Spirit). In verse 5, we see that there are varieties of *ministries*, but the same Lord (Jesus is Lord over all whom He uses as His instruments in various ministries, such as the ministry of healing or prophecy). In verse 6, we see that there are varieties of *effects*, or results, and it is God who oversees these results. In verse 7, we see that "to each one is given the manifestation of the Spirit for the common good."

So, these gifts belong to the Holy Spirit and not to individual Christians. Christians are not able to operate in the gifts whenever they want to. Paul was a Christian who was used many times to deliver gifts of healings to those who needed it. Yet, he was not able to bring healing to Trophimus. Paul wrote, ". . . But Trophimus I left sick at Miletus" (II Timothy 4:20). We do not know why Trophimus was not healed. This is God's responsibility, and not ours.

A brief analysis of the wonderful healing described in Acts 3 should prove helpful. In Acts 3:1–8, we see the ministry to a man who was lame from birth (verse 2) and who was now forty years old (see Acts 4: 22). He had never walked. His legs had no functioning muscles; consequently, they were probably very undeveloped and weak. Since he sat at the gate of the temple every day, Jesus had certainly walked past him many times, without healing him, because in the divine wisdom of the Trinity, it was not yet time for his healing (see John 9:1–5).

As Peter and John approached the lame man who was sitting by the gate, Peter's attention and his gaze were drawn to him. In the moment before Peter spoke to the man, the Holy Spirit must have done several things. First, He gave Peter a "word of knowledge" (I Corinthians 12:8), saying that He was going to heal that man. Upon receiving such a word from the Holy Spirit, many Christians would question whether they had heard correctly from the Lord. Instead of trusting in that word from the Lord, they might ask the man if it would be all right for them to pray for his legs and then just see what God would do. Instead, Peter believed the word of knowledge.

The second thing the Spirit did was to give the manifestational gift of faith (verse 9). This caused Peter to become absolutely certain that this man's legs would be healed. One could hardly imagine telling a man with shriveled-up legs to stand up and walk unless he was given this supernatural gift of faith.

The Holy Spirit gave Peter the prompting to give the man a command, and as Peter commanded the man to stand up and walk, the manifestational gifts of healings and miracles (verses 9 and 10) were both released into this man's body. Peter delivered these gifts from God to this man by giving the command. God created new muscles, new arteries and veins, new nerves, and He caused these legs to function normally, suddenly. The man stood and began walking and leaping and praising God (Acts 3:8). Surely he talked about it for the rest of his life. This miracle had a profound effect on many, and the church was strengthened as believers became more aware of how much God loved them and realized that He was prepared to enter into their lives supernaturally.

This instance of healing in Acts 3 was not one in which the person who received healing had great faith for his healing, such as the woman who touched the Lord's cloak (see Matthew 9:20–22). She had great faith, and Jesus said to her, "Your faith has made you well." In Mark 2:1–12, we read of a paralytic who was carried to Jesus and was healed. It was the faith of those who carried him that was instrumental in his healing (see verse 5).

How can we who are not apostles, as Peter was, be the deliverers of God's miraculous gifts? Jesus said that it is *those who believe in Him* who would do the works that He did. "He who believes in Me [Jesus], the works that I do shall he do also; and greater works than these shall he do; because I go to the Father" (John 14:12).

The Lord knows that we cannot see into the spiritual realm like He can (see I Corinthians 13:12), but He has taught us that "if you have faith as a mustard seed, you shall say to this mountain, 'Move from here to there,' and it shall move; and nothing shall be impossible to you" (Matthew 17:20). As I see it, this means that if we believe *He* can do the miraculous thing that is before us, and if we believe *He* is prompting us to pray for it, that is enough to constitute "faith as a mustard seed." We can then pray boldly for the thing before us. This amounts to us joining with Him in the Father's work (see John 5:19).

The gift of prophecy is much simpler than most people imagine. Many Christians believe prophecy is predicting the future. While it is true that a fair amount of prophecy in the Old Testament had to do with what was to come, this was often because of what had already happened among the Israelites, and the future events were the consequences of their previous choices, which were not pleasing to God. When Jesus established the New Covenant, all believers were given the Holy Spirit and were enabled to deliver a prophetic word for God. God began to give more prophecies more often through His children.

He used Paul to describe for us what prophecy is. We read in I Corinthians 14:3 that "one who prophesies speaks to men for edification and exhortation and consolation." When the Holy Spirit sees that a person, a family, or a group needs edification, exhortation or consolation, He will look for a faithful believer whom He can use to deliver such a helpful, prophetic word. Prophecy is not just human encouragement. It is a divine, supernatural gift from God.

Here is an example of how the gift of prophecy can be manifested today. Steve and Karen were trying to adopt a child from a foreign country, and the red tape had frustrated them for more than six months. They had become discouraged. One Sunday morning, while getting ready to come to church where I was serving, Steve said to Karen, "Honey, I believe God has forgotten us." She said she agreed.

In silence they drove to the church with their two boys, Mark and Charles. They were in great need. During the service, just as I was getting ready to enter into the pastoral prayer, the Lord gave me a word of knowledge about a need for healing in the congregation. I didn't know who had the need. I spoke out the word of knowledge: "Someone here has pain in your left eye, and it really hurts. God is saying that if you will turn to Him and ask Him to heal it, He will heal it right now, during the service." Mark had just been complaining to his dad that his left eye was really hurting. Steve had been short with him, telling him to be quiet. When Steve heard the word of knowledge, he said to his son, Mark, "Well, are you going to ask God to heal your eye?" Mark said, "Yes." God healed his eye within a few seconds after he asked for the healing.

After the service, Steve brought Mark up front to speak to me. I had no idea whose left eye had been hurting, so it was a real blessing for me to hear the report that God had healed Mark's eye. I said something like "praise the Lord." Then, from down inside me came these words from God: "See there, Steve, God has not forgotten you" (this was a prophetic word of encouragement).

Steve began to weep. I didn't know why, since I knew nothing of his earlier conversation with Karen, when they had agreed that God had forgotten them. Then Steve turned and walked straight over to Karen and told her what had happened. They held each other and wept with joy, because of the prophetic word of encouragement that they had received. Within a few weeks, their adopted child was safely in their arms.

God also may give words of prophecy like this to people who are not yet Christians. Such a word will often prepare a person to receive Christ. I recommend *The Beginner's Guide to the Gift of Prophecy,* by Jack Deere.

The account that I reported above documented the delivery of three of the manifestational gifts: the gift of the word of knowledge, the gift of healing, and the gift of prophecy. I was the available vessel whom God chose to use to deliver those gifts in order to bless that family. I have been used before to deliver the gifts of healing and prophecy and many times have delivered the gift of the word of knowledge. I don't carry those gifts with me. I just remain aware that God might prompt me to deliver a gift, especially in a setting in which the Holy Spirit is moving among His people.

God still delights in showing His own children, and this lost world, that He is prepared to do supernatural things for people because He loves them.

CHAPTER TWELVE

His Desire to Use Believers in Ministry

Just before Jesus ascended to the right hand of the Father (see Acts 1:9, Hebrews 10:12), He said to His disciples, "You shall receive power when the Holy Spirit has come upon you, and you shall be My witnesses both in Jerusalem, and in all Judea and Samaria, and even to the remotest part of the earth" (Acts 1:8). Many people have interpreted this Scripture in a limited way, believing that it refers only to evangelism. While evangelism is certainly encouraged in this passage, we must also consider Jesus' last words in Matthew 28:19: "Go therefore and make disciples of all the nations . . . ."

In order to make a disciple, one must first present the Gospel and help the person receive Christ. The next step is ". . . teaching them to observe all that I commanded you . . ." (Matthew 28:20). We must understand that the call of Jesus Christ on every believer's life is to minister to others, in various ways, as He directs. Our motivation to carry out this ministry to others is love as described in the Great Commandment, where we are called to love God and love our neighbors as ourselves (Matthew 22:37–39).

Ephesians 2:10 is an extremely important Scripture that is often overlooked: "We are His workmanship, created in Christ Jesus for good works, which God prepared beforehand, that we should walk in them." Let's consider this verse in its parts.

- *"We are His workmanship"*: God made us new creatures when we were born again (II Corinthians 5:17), so we are His workmanship. We belong to Him as a pot belongs to its maker. We are no longer separated from Him, but are loved by Him and invited to join Him in His glorious works here on the earth.
- *"Created in Christ Jesus for good works"*: We are made to be conformed to the image of His Son, Jesus (Romans 8:29), equipped with God's Holy Spirit, and called to do "works" that He calls "good." While this calling can lead us to serve on a committee or a board, it usually will mean that we are to minister to people directly, as He leads us.
- *"Which God prepared beforehand"*: When God arranged for us to be called by Jesus to minister in various ways, He had specific things already in mind for each of us to do—enough to last a lifetime.
- *"That we should walk in them"*: God will show us when to step out in ministry and what He wants us to do. God will prepare the way for the ministry He has for us to do, and He will empower us to do it just the way He wants it to be done. Our part is to remain aware of God's plan to do this, listening for the Holy Spirit's prompting and then obeying that prompting.

Before I began to serve the Lord as a pastor, I worked in the business world. At one time, I had made a change and was in a new job in a new part of Atlanta. I was just getting my new desk the way I wanted it when I sensed in my spirit that the Holy Spirit was prompting me to "call Bill." At first I couldn't discern who "Bill" was. Then I remembered.

Bill was a man whom I had met some time back. We had lost touch with each other, and I wasn't sure what he was doing. Then, I thought, "I must not have been hearing the Lord. Must have been just me." I pushed the thought away.

Then, in my spirit, I heard the instruction again: "Call Bill." I sought confirmation from the Lord and sensed that He really was prompting me to call Bill.

I argued with God, saying, "But I don't really have a reason to call him. I don't know what to say. I'll look like a fool." The words "call Bill" came to mind again.

"Okay, Lord." So, I called Bill.

When he answered the phone, I said, "Hi, Bill. It's Dick Robinson. I thought I'd just check and see how you're doing."

He nearly shouted into the phone—and my ear—as he said, "Dick, how did you know that I was trying to find you so I could call you? I really need to talk with you. I've got a problem that I think you can help me with."

We talked for about thirty minutes, and I was able to help him. He felt better. I was elated that I had been given the privilege of helping him find his answer. God really knew what He was doing. He knew Bill's problem, and He knew Bill was trying to reach me. God knew that it would be very fulfilling for me to be able to help Bill. He blessed me in this way. The Lord opened the door for me to join Him in doing something in Bill's life, and I will probably never learn the end of the story. That's okay. It was a privilege to do my part.

In Acts chapter 8, we read how the church was scattered beyond Jerusalem, and the Lord's disciples were preaching the Gospel where God had sent them. God sent Philip to Samaria and prepared the way for him there (see Acts 8:4–8). As he preached, the people were captivated, because the

Holy Spirit was working in their minds and hearts. As Philip ministered to the people, God did miraculous things (signs).

The Holy Spirit used Philip to minister supernatural healing, and people who were lame or paralyzed were healed. Philip cast demons out of people. The Lord was glorified, and the people rejoiced. Certainly, Philip experienced much joy himself as he saw what God did through his simple obedience. He probably would have been very happy to continue ministering in that place for quite some time to come, but God had other plans for him.

We see in Acts 8:26 that God spoke to Philip through an angel and told him to go south to the road that led to Gaza. God did not tell Philip why He was sending him there. Many Christians today would have been reluctant to leave the exciting ministry in Samaria and either would have denied that they had actually encountered that angel or simply would have disobeyed the word of the Lord to them. Philip obeyed.

When Philip arrived at the road, he saw an Ethiopian eunuch in a chariot. Then the Spirit of the Lord told Philip to join the eunuch in his chariot (Acts 8:27–40). Apparently God did not tell Philip why He was sending him to the eunuch. Philip simply obeyed the Holy Spirit's instruction.

The Holy Spirit guided and empowered Philip in his ministry to the eunuch, and the eunuch became a Christian and was baptized. The work of the Holy Spirit in this situation was not manifested only in Philip's life. The Spirit had been at work in the eunuch, drawing him to read the words of the prophet Isaiah and preparing his heart for the moment when the Lord would lift the veil from his eyes (see II Corinthians 4:3–4, 6) and draw him into the Kingdom.

This biblical account may seem somewhat dramatic, and modern-day Christians may think that God does not do this sort of thing today. However, God *is* actively at work among a great number of modern-day Christians who are willing to receive Jesus' call on their lives and who recognize that God's almighty Holy Spirit lives in them and is eager to use them in ministry. These are obedient Christians who are relatively free of "the fear of man" (Proverbs 29:25). They do not walk in fear of what people will think or say when their obedience to the Lord might appear to be somewhat "unusual." They would rather please God than please man.

When the Holy Spirit prompts us to draw near to another person, we will usually know that it is the Spirit who is prompting us. That person may need salvation, encouragement, healing, a prayer partner, or even correction. Whatever may be the case, if God is prompting us to draw near to someone, He also is preparing that person's heart to receive our ministry.

That person needs the ministry that the Holy Spirit wants to offer through us. The Lord will show us how to approach him or her in a caring way, with love and humility. When that individual receives God's ministry through us, he will be blessed, God will be glorified, and we will be blessed as well. God wants to hear from us. He wants to know that we are ready to serve Him in the ministry that He has for us.

CHAPTER THIRTEEN

His Omnipresence and His Manifest Presence

From the beginning, the Christian church has believed that God is present everywhere in the universe. In Psalm 139:7, King David asked God these questions: "Where can I go from Thy Spirit? Or where can I flee from Thy presence?" In Jeremiah 23:24, the prophet writes: " 'Can a man hide himself in hiding places, so I do not see him?' declares the Lord. 'Do I not fill the heavens and the earth?' declares the Lord." Since God created this vast universe, He is certainly as large as the universe and simultaneously has dominion over all parts of it. Christians take comfort in knowing that God is everywhere. We can know this because Scripture tells us this, and the Holy Spirit can confirm it to us in our spirits.

King David was fervent about giving thanks to God. In his "psalm of gratitude," he wrote, "Tell of His glory among the nations, His wonderful deeds among all the peoples" (I Chronicles 16:24). He wanted to give glory to God, and he also wanted testimony to be given about the mighty deeds of the God of Israel, so that the people could continually be encouraged to trust God as their Protector and Provider.

Most of the people of Israel believed that God was every-where—omnipresent. However, God was *very* present on the day that He parted the Red Sea, performing this "wonderful deed among all the peoples" (see Exodus 14:21–22). As the people of Israel crossed through the Red Sea on dry land, the water stood up like walls on either side of them. This was a mighty act of God, the Holy Spirit. This was a time when the Holy Spirit's presence and power were shown, or made manifest, to all who were there. This was His manifest presence.

When God met Moses and the people of Israel at Mt. Sinai, they experienced His manifest presence (Exodus 19:16–19). The mountain shook violently, and there was a "thick cloud" upon it. Smoke ascended from the mountain "like smoke of a furnace," because the Lord "descended upon it in fire!" There were "thunder and lightning flashes and . . . a very loud trumpet sound, so that all the people who were in the camp trembled." They were afraid for their lives. The Holy Spirit has the power to shake a mountain or a man, or He can touch a man gently, like the time He had Moses put his hand into his robe and when Moses drew out his hand, it was leprous. When God told Moses to put his hand back into his robe and pull it out once more, Moses' hand was healed (Exodus 4:6–7).

The manifest presence of the Holy Spirit has been active every time a miracle from God has occurred. When Jesus told Peter to cast his fishing net on the other side of his boat (John 21:6) and the net came up full of fish, this was the result of the manifest presence of the Holy Spirit at work. When the lame man at the gate of the temple was healed (Acts 3:1–8), the manifest presence of the Holy Spirit was at work. In Acts 4:23–31, when the early church was gathered and they cried out, asking God to continue to glorify Himself through signs and wonders, "the place where they had gathered together was shaken, and they were all filled with the Holy Spirit, and began to speak the Word of God with boldness." Again, the manifest presence of the Holy Spirit was displayed.

In these modern times, in those places where Christians want to serve God in the power of the Holy Spirit and they believe God wants to move in power to bless people and glorify Himself, the manifest presence of God is being experienced frequently with healings and other evidences of God's power at work. This powerful spiritual atmosphere in such places is glorifying God and resulting in the salvation of many people. God's Kingdom is growing.

In Psalm 22:3, King David wrote, "Yet Thou art holy, O Thou who art enthroned upon the praises of Israel." As a musician (I Samuel 16:17–19), David knew that the manifest presence of the Holy Spirit would come as he worshiped God fervently with his harp. Today, when worship leaders in a church service go beyond "performing" and on into personal worship, God's people are encouraged to release themselves into worship. The Holy Spirit is pleased to come and enthrone Himself in the praises of these people. They can sense God's presence. He is there offering His power for ministry. If prayer ministry is offered after the service, frequently powerful works of God are seen. The Holy Spirit wants to come in His manifest presence, as we invite Him through our praise and worship and pray for people in response to His prompting.

In 1975 I was in a church service one Sunday evening in Atlanta, where a visiting speaker was expected. We were worshiping in a wonderful atmosphere of surrender to God when we got word that the speaker's flight had been delayed and that he might be as much as an hour late. The host pastor asked the crowd what they wanted to do. We let him know that we wanted to continue to worship. He said, "Good. Let's worship."

As we continued to worship God, many who were there, including myself, began to feel the presence of the Holy

Spirit. When the visiting speaker appeared on the platform, he stood there for a moment. Then he said, "The presence of the Lord is here in great power. He is here with power to heal. I believe that if we just continue to worship Him, He is just going to begin to heal people."

I believe that in addition to sensing the presence of the Lord spiritually, this speaker had received a word of knowledge from the Lord that He was going to be healing people. We continued to worship the Lord, and soon people began to cry out, "It's gone. I'm healed. The pain is gone. I can move my shoulder now!" A man who was standing right in front of me brought his right arm up and slapped the back of his neck and shouted, "It's gone! Praise the Lord!" I believe I heard the cries of about twelve to fifteen people, exclaiming that they had been healed . . . and nobody had prayed for them. God was just healing people by the moving of the Holy Spirit. That evening, we experienced the manifest presence of the Holy Spirit.

A pastor friend, who for more than thirty years had served a variety of challenging, small, country churches in which family feuds often end up hurting the pastor, had come to a place where he was just worn out. He had grown up in the beautiful mountains of North Carolina, but now he was heartsick over some of the things he had witnessed during his pastoral ministry. He was almost sixty years old, and he had serious pain in each shoulder joint as a result of problems in his rotator cuffs. He couldn't even reach up to get a glass from the cupboard. He felt somewhat depressed and simply wasn't very happy. Out of secret savings for her husband, his wife was able to provide for him a trip to a particular church where the Holy Spirit was moving in great power and touching and healing people. She knew he needed to go there.

The first evening, after participating in glorious worship and sensing the Holy Spirit moving powerfully, he went forward for prayer. While he was being prayed for, the Holy Spirit overwhelmed him with peace, like anesthesia. He slumped to the floor and lay there in a heavy blanket of God's peace, a peace that was deeper than he had ever felt before.

He was conscious of his surroundings, but he didn't particularly care what was happening around him. This was a very special time with the Lord. After about fifteen minutes of the flood of peace, he began to weep. Soon he began to sob, as the Holy Spirit began to minister to his deep hurts. After about ten minutes of sobbing, the pain left, and he was flooded with peace once again. His wounds had been healed. After another fifteen minutes of peace, he broke into laughter . . . loud laughter. There was nothing funny going on. God was ministering joy to his joy-deprived heart. When that was over, he was again flooded with peace.

Then he heard the Lord say, "Danny, do you remember when you were a boy in the mountains, and you would fall back into the snow bank and make a snow angel?"

"Yes, Sir."

"Danny, make a snow angel there on the carpet."

"But, Lord, my shoulders. They are messed up and hurt too much . . ."

"Danny, make a snow angel."

So, Danny made a snow angel there on the carpet, raising his arms above his head easily. He experienced no pain. Both shoulders had been completely healed by the ministry of the Holy Spirit. Nobody had prayed for his shoulders to be healed. God's love had prevailed and touched this man of God. Danny had been overshadowed by the manifest presence of the Holy Spirit.

CHAPTER FOURTEEN

Baptized With the Holy Spirit

For a hundred years, Bible scholars and theologians have discussed, with some intensity, the phrase "baptized with the Holy Spirit." Pentecostals, orthodox evangelicals, and others have expressed different interpretations of what the phrase means, as well as the theological implications of what application of those interpretations might mean for the church. I want to present what I believe to be a biblical position regarding the phrase "baptized with the Holy Spirit."

First, I want to establish the foundation upon which my position is built and the context in which it is to be understood. God has graciously saved us, given us eternal life, made us His children, and called us into service. Being in His service is not just "church-sponsored service." It involves the very way we live our lives, which becomes a testimony before the world, before our church family, and before our family at home.

God has called us to live lives that are extraordinary — not as the world lives. He has called us to live supernatural lives. How can He expect us to do that? He expects that because He has placed His Holy Spirit inside us, in our hearts (Galatians 4:6), to empower, control, and guide our lives. Since the Holy Spirit is the third Person of the Trinity, He is God, just as the Father and the Son are God. This means that He is a supernatural being and has all the sovereign power and wisdom that the other two Persons in the Trinity have.

God has plans for each of His children, plans that serve His purposes, that bless others, and that give all of us who walk in His plans deep satisfaction and fulfillment. When He saved us, we became His workmanship, created in Christ Jesus for good works, which He prepared beforehand so that we could have the privilege and joy of serving Him (Ephesians 2:10). This is exciting news for those of us who really love God and want to be His servants. How can we do this? How can we know what it is He wants us to do, and how can we manage to do it for Him?

If we are willing to be God's instruments, His Holy Spirit will show us—reveal to us—what He wants us to do, usually around the time He wants us to do it. If we really want to be His instruments and to be used by God to bring blessings to others and thus glorify our Lord Jesus, we will do our best to remain alert to the work of the Holy Spirit inside us as He shows us truth.

As He draws our attention to a particular person or situation, He will give us an understanding of a need in that situation or in that person's life and then give us His "nudge," indicating that He wants us to step up and be a part of His solution to that need. It may take some courage to respond to that nudge, because it may take us outside of our comfort zone. It will take faith to live this way. It will take faith to believe that God will send us on such a mission, that He will let us know it is time to step out and enter into the situation, and that He will give us the knowledge, wisdom, and the empowering by the Holy Spirit to do the work that He will call us to do.

When we *do* step out in obedience and faith, He *does* provide all the guidance and empowering that is needed for that which He has called us to do. When we first begin to

live these supernatural lives, He does not give us assign-
ments that are overwhelming, such as parting the Red Sea.
He knows that we are beginners in this supernatural life. He
may call us simply to love someone.

He has poured His supernatural *agape* love into our
hearts by the Holy Spirit, who lives in us (see Romans 5:5).
If we will make ourselves vulnerable to Him and willingly
take the risk of being a channel of His supernatural love for
someone He has pointed us to, His work will bring amazing
results. His Word says that He prepared this work beforehand (Ephesians 2:10). This means not only that God has
had it in His mind for a while, but also that He goes before us
to prepare that person's heart to receive the ministry of love
that He has called us to carry out.

Not many weeks after my wife Carrie and I entered into
this supernatural life, the Holy Spirit asked us to take into
our home a miserable, ungrateful, penniless, nineteen-year-
old girl who was nine months pregnant. We did not know
His plans for her. We just felt impressed in our hearts that He
wanted us to meet her need for a place to stay, for a time (as
it turned out, she was with us for four months). After she had
moved into our home, we found out that she was a Jehovah's
Witness and that she smoked (I'm very allergic to cigarette
smoke). We cried, "O Lord, what do you want us to do with
this girl?" We sensed He was saying that He just wanted us
to love her with His love.

"O Lord, she is not very lovable. We need You to fill us
with Your love for her." He did just that. We were amazed.
This was an Ephesians 2:10 thing. She responded to God's
love as He flowed through us, and she began to warm up
to us. Pretty soon, she wanted us to have Bible study with
her every night. This provided an opportunity to give her
the truth. In two weeks, she burned the Jehovah's Witness
books that she had held onto since childhood. In another two
weeks, she prayed with us to receive Jesus as her Savior and

Lord. Before she left, God had set her free from her addiction to cigarettes. While she was with us she had her baby, and this provided the opportunity for Carrie to teach her how to be the mother of a newborn.

The work that was done in this girl's heart was all God's doing. We couldn't do any of it. Our willingness to love her for God just provided the "lubricant" for the work of the Holy Spirit as He did several supernatural things in her life: (1) Changed her mind about the Jehovah's Witness cult, (2) saved her soul, and (3) set her free from cigarettes (she just woke up one morning without any desire for a cigarette).

Being involved in this kind of Godly activity and getting to watch and see what God is doing and then joining with Him in that work is what living the supernatural life is all about. We want to take God up on His invitation to join Him in a part of the wondrous work He is doing all over the earth. Jesus said that the works He does, we will do also, and we will do even greater things (John 14:12). If we want to be involved in opportunities like this, we will want to join God in what He is doing as the Holy Spirit gives us His invitation to join Him (see John 5:19).

You may ask, "How does one enter into this supernatural life?" It is simpler than you might think. It is mostly a matter of complete surrender to God's Holy Spirit. Many Christians believe they fully surrendered to the Holy Spirit when they received Jesus as their Savior and Lord. They know that the Holy Spirit entered them at the moment they received Jesus, and it seems logical to them that their lives would now be surrendered to the Holy Spirit.

If this were really true, the Apostle Paul would not have seen the need to warn Christians about *quenching* the Holy Spirit (I Thessalonians 5:19) or *grieving* the Holy Spirit (Ephesians 4:30). These are two ways that modern Christians seriously disappoint God, because of our lack of full surrender. Here are some examples: (1) When I am afraid that my friend is offending the person in front of us by sharing the Gospel with him, and I step up and change the subject, I am probably *quenching* the Holy Spirit. (2) When I commit sin, as a result of my own selfishness, I am *grieving* the Holy Spirit. (3) When I sense that God is nudging me to go over and talk to that lonely person, and I refuse to do it, I am *resisting* the Holy Spirit (Acts 7:51). Any one who does any serious and honest reflection on his life can see how he has done each of these kinds of things because of a lack of surrender to the Holy Spirit.

God wants to do so much in the earth today through His people. He wants the world to know that His entry into their lives changed their lives and that they became temples of His Holy Spirit. However, many Christians don't live lives that are surrendered to the Holy Spirit because they are either too busy with their own programs, afraid to let the Holy Spirit take charge, afraid of possible rejection by their Christian peers or leadership, or convinced that the Holy Spirit is no longer active in the earth today. Our wonderful, loving, supernatural God wants us to be bold for Him as we remain alert to the nudges of His Holy Spirit, willing to step out into His service when He calls us, no matter what obstacle may loom before us.

He wants us to be bold like the Christians who cried out, "Lord, take note of their threats, and grant that Thy bond-servants may speak Thy word with all confidence, while Thou dost extend Thy hand to heal, and signs and wonders take place through the name of Thy holy servant Jesus" (Acts 4:29–31). This Godly boldness is not zeal without wisdom. It is a willingness to serve God when He calls, regardless of whether this obedience may take us out of our circle of comfort or confidence.

A heart that is really surrendered, trusting in God and eager to serve Him, will receive a holy boldness and the leading of His Holy Spirit and His wisdom. This servant will receive clear guidance and will be empowered to confront any obstacles that he encounters in the path of obedience. In order for the supernatural work of the Holy Spirit to be fully active in a person's life, he or she needs to intentionally make a decision to totally surrender to the empowering and control of the Holy Spirit by being baptized with the Holy Spirit. Let's examine this concept of being baptized with the Holy Spirit.

John the Baptist said of Jesus, "I baptize you with water for repentance, but He who is coming after me is mightier than I, and I am not fit to remove His sandals; He will baptize you with the Holy Spirit and fire" (Matthew 3:11; see also Mark 1:8, Luke 3:16, and John 1:33). So, Jesus is the One who baptizes with the Holy Spirit.

In Acts 1:1–5, Luke describes how Jesus appeared to the disciples for forty days, following the resurrection. Then, He gathered them together and told them not to leave Jerusalem until they had been baptized with the Holy Spirit "not many days from now." The traditional orthodox church has believed, for some time, that God gave the Holy Spirit to the disciples on the Day of Pentecost. However, some important Scriptures have not been fully considered.

In John 7:39, Jesus said that those who believe in Him were to receive the Holy Spirit (future tense) for the Spirit was not yet given, because Jesus was not yet glorified. In order to discover when the Holy Spirit was given to Jesus' disciples, we must ask ourselves, When was Jesus glorified? One position held is that He was glorified when He was taken up into Heaven (Acts 1:9). However, Scripture does not say that.

The disciples were totally crestfallen after Jesus was crucified and put into the tomb. Their leader, their hope, was now dead. He had said that He was the Son of God and that He could defeat even death, but where was He?

Then, the day of the resurrection came, resulting in events that have impacted the human race for nearly two thousand years. Romans 1:4 states that He was "declared with power to be the Son of God by the resurrection from the dead, according to the Spirit of holiness, Jesus Christ our Lord." It was His resurrection that glorified Him. Without this resurrection, none of us would have eternal life today. The resurrection occurred fifty days before Pentecost Sunday and forty days before the account recorded in Acts 1:1–5.

John 20:19–22 records the account of the resurrected Lord Jesus' appearance in the midst of His disciples. They rejoiced at seeing Him. After declaring that He was sending them even as the Father had sent Him, Jesus breathed on them and said, "Receive the Holy Spirit." The word *receive* is in the Greek imperative tense. It is a command. Jesus imparted the Holy Spirit to His disciples at this time.

As the Holy Spirit entered them, they were regenerated. They were born again and given eternal life. Prior to this time, they hadn't understood His parables very well, because it is the Holy Spirit who enables us to understand the things of God, and they had not yet received Him (see I Corinthians 2:12–14).

Modern commentaries struggle to explain John 20:22. Some of them ignore this verse, and some of them suggest that Jesus gave His disciples "a sprinkling of the Holy Spirit" and that the rest of the Holy Spirit came on the Day of Pentecost, or some other explanation. This verse seems clear to me. In the Greek imperative tense, Jesus said, "Receive the Holy Spirit." They received the Holy Spirit and were regenerated, or born again. That is what the Holy Spirit does when He comes into a person.

Jesus' disciples had been learning with Jesus for about three years. They had received the Great Commission (Matthew 28:18–20) after His resurrection, and they were eager to go out into the world. However, forty days after the resurrection, He met with them and said, "Wait." They had the Holy Spirit in them, but there was more for them. They were to be baptized with the Holy Spirit "not many days from now" (Acts 1:5).

One of the problems that some have with the term "baptized with the Holy Spirit" is that the use of the word *baptized* makes it sound like a sacrament. Being baptized with the Holy Spirit is not a sacrament. Jesus used the word *baptized* in Acts 1:5, in the same way John the Baptist used it to say that Jesus would "baptize" us with the Holy Spirit.

In first-century Greek, *baptizo* (which means "I baptize") was a word normally used in the marketplace to mean "to immerse, to overwhelm with something, to soak, to plunge into." If you went to the market to buy a cloak, you might well find merchants selling wool cloaks in their natural wool shades, waiting for a buyer to select a dye color of his choice. If the buyer indicated that he wanted a red cloak, the merchant would most likely plunge the new cloak into a vat of red dye and manipulate it in the vat with a long pole. The cloak would be baptized, or soaked through and through, with the red dye. The merchant would be the baptizer.

When the baptizer took the cloak out of the dye, it would be the same cloak, but it would also be a different cloak. It would have the same shape, but its appearance would have changed, because the element in which it was baptized would have fully penetrated every thread. The cloak did not resist being overwhelmed by the element in which it was baptized. Instead, it received and "soaked up" the element in which it was baptized. Now, simply by observing it, anyone would be able to discern that the robe had been baptized in red dye.

The Holy Spirit already lives in the human spirit or heart of every Christian (see Romans 8:9, and refer again to Galatians 4:6). When Jesus baptizes a believer in His Holy Spirit, there is a flooding of the soul (mind, will, and emotions) by the Holy Spirit, as the believer surrenders to Him.

Jesus baptizes with the Holy Spirit those people who are very much in love with Him, people who are eager to surrender to the Holy Spirit and become Spirit-filled servants (see Ephesians 5:18), no matter what the Holy Spirit may ask of them. They know that the Holy Spirit is God, and therefore He can be trusted (just like they trust Jesus). They know that He will do with them only those things that are right. These believers have come to the place where they are willing to be truly vulnerable to the Holy Spirit.

These surrendered believers want the Holy Spirit to fully develop His fruit in them (Galatians 5:22–23), and they are willing for the Spirit to impart any of His gifts through them (I Corinthians 12:4–11). Some of the supernatural gifts may seem a little bit scary. However, just remember that the work of the Holy Spirit, which caused us to be born again, was a powerful, supernatural work, and we are surely grateful to God for that supernatural work of His Spirit! Be assured that God's motive in the use of all of His supernatural gifts is His love for His church, His children that are in His church, and those unsaved ones who are not yet in His church (John 10:16).

A bit of testimony: I was saved out of an unchurched background at age thirty-two and was intensely grateful to God for His forgiveness and the gift of eternal life. I wanted to serve Him with all of my heart. I began a life of prayer, Bible study, and "doing good." I did not understand how much the Holy Spirit (who already lived in me) wanted to fill me, guide me, and empower me, so that I could live the supernatural life. Instead, I thought I had to do it myself—with my strength, my wisdom, and my resources—and that He would be there to "help" me somehow.

After about four years of working hard in my own strength, an elder discerned that I was near "Christian burnout." I had begun to be a little bit "cranky" about all that I now had to do (which I had volunteered to do, incidentally). This elder asked me to have lunch with him. I said, "Sure, but what is on your mind?"

He said, "I can see how much you love the Lord and how you want to serve Him and glorify Him, but you are doing it in your own strength. You are probably near burnout. I want to put you out of your misery."

"Out of my misery? How so?"

"I want to share with you how to let the Holy Spirit take over and empower you."

In the course of our lunch, he explained what Paul tells us in Ephesians 5:18—that we are to be filled with the Holy Spirit. Christians that are filled are often called "Spirit-filled" Christians. This means they are controlled and empowered by the Holy Spirit. I liked the "empowered by" part, but I never liked the idea of being controlled by anyone. I had to come to the conclusion that since I really trusted God the Father and Jesus the Son, I also could trust the Holy Spirit. I could trust Him to do only things that were right for me, even if I didn't fully understand them and even if I didn't like them.

Some of the people in the church I was attending had an uneasy feeling about their fellow members who seemed so interested in the things of the Holy Spirit. These people did not know much about Him and had received "teaching via conversation" from relatives and friends who strongly suggested that there was something strange about the workings of the Holy Spirit. I was in a Presbyterian church, and there were people among us who spoke negatively about the Pentecostals, describing them as people who often seemed unnecessarily emotional in their worship and in the way they talked about God. There seemed to be a "low-grade fear" about this, since these church members had been taught that we were to do things "decently, and in order" when it concerned the things of God. They seemed to believe there was a link between the Holy Spirit and emotionalism. I was kind of reserved myself, and so I experienced some of that same uneasiness, especially when my senior pastor said that I should "be careful" around those people.

However, when I began to consider the elder who wanted to introduce me to this way of living in the fullness of the Holy Spirit, I realized that he was sort of reserved, like me, except that the love of Jesus constantly radiated from his face. He was a man who manifested the fruit of the Holy Spirit like few men I had ever met. He also was a man who had the courage to pray and ask God to heal people. He seemed to understand that he didn't have to carry the responsibility for the final outcome of these "God encounters" that the Lord let him participate in. That was God's business. This man's role was simply that of a servant. He had only to pray, share, love, or do whatever God nudged him to do and then let God be responsible for the outcome.

At the beginning of this discussion on the concept of being "baptized with the Holy Spirit," I mentioned the need to adequately consider the Scriptures involved. Now we need to look more carefully at I Corinthians 12:13: "For by one Spirit we were all baptized into one body, whether Jews or Greeks, whether slaves or free, and we were all made to drink of one Spirit." This verse has been quoted by some as evidence that we are all baptized with the Holy Spirit as a part of being saved. Some people propose that this verse presents the very same message given by John the Baptist, recorded in Matthew 3:11, and the message of Jesus, recorded in Acts 1:5. It is clear to me that being baptized into the Body of Christ is a wonderful thing, because it signifies that the Holy Spirit places us—immerses us—into His wonderful family. The verse also says, "We were all made to drink of one Spirit." This would seem to indicate that we all received the Holy Spirit into our bodies (which have now become temples of the Holy Spirit). Also, in Romans 8:9 we learn that if we belong to Christ, we have His Spirit.

In order to be clear, we need to remember that according to John the Baptist's declaration, Jesus would baptize us with the Holy Spirit, Jesus is the Baptizer, and we are baptized into the Holy Spirit. In I Corinthians 12:13, we learn that the Holy Spirit is the Baptizer and that we are baptized into the Body of Christ. So, the two statements are really different; they do not say the same thing. The two statements refer to two different things, two different events.

The issue that seems most troubling to many is the idea that there is an additional, or deeper way, to relate to, or with, the Holy Spirit, beyond the blessed privilege of having Him living inside of our spirits, dwelling within us. It is my observation that the disciples received the Holy Spirit on the eve of the resurrection, so that He was then dwelling within them, and then they had an additional experience with Him on the Day of Pentecost. Jesus referred to this additional experience as being "baptized with the Holy Spirit." Therefore, it seems that there really is a deeper relationship with the Holy Spirit available to us. It is one of a continual posture of surrender to Him, and it follows an initial, conscious decision to surrender.

Let's consider Jesus' instructions to His disciples in Acts 1. These men were excited about serving their risen Lord. Following His resurrection, they saw His miraculous work again, when He told them to cast the net on the right side of the boat (John 21:6), and they caught so many fish they could not haul them all into the boat. This miracle occurred after they had been fishing all night but had not caught any fish. Then, after gathering His disciples, in the Acts 1 account Jesus told them not to leave Jerusalem but to wait until they had been "baptized with the Holy Spirit not many days from now." He was referring to this coming event when He said, in verse 8, "You shall receive power when the Holy Spirit has come upon you; and you shall be My witnesses . . . ."

As I reflect on the modern-day church's efforts at witnessing to the lost, I see a great lack of power, boldness, and wisdom. I can only assume that not many of God's people have sought this empowering of the Holy Spirit, probably largely because they have not understood what I am sharing in this chapter.

The disciples were obedient and waited in the "upper room" in Jerusalem (Acts 1:13). They entered into what I call a "ten-day prayer meeting" (from the fortieth day after the resurrection to the fiftieth day, the Day of Pentecost). I've never been in a ten-day prayer meeting, but I imagine that it would be quite an experience.

Based on our understanding that they were eager to go forth and serve Him, we can easily surmise that they might have begun by praying that Jesus would baptize them with the Holy Spirit. My guess is that as time passed in this prayer meeting, the Lord made them aware of their own self-sufficiency—their own independent ways and selfishness—and showed them that they had to give up all their self-sufficiency. He may have reminded them of His words: "Apart from Me, you can do nothing" (John 15:5).

Most likely, He brought them to a serious level of surrender, as when a grain of wheat falls into the earth and dies (John 12:23–25), in which they had to acknowledge the bankruptcy of their former way of life and become simply His sheep, His little children, His servants, willing for Him to do whatever He wanted to do in their lives. This level of surrender prepares us to be baptized with the Holy Spirit—filled, controlled, directed, empowered for the supernatural life—in which we are less and He is lots more, so that when wonderful things happen in conjunction with our simple servant obedience, He gets the glory, not us.

If this discussion has caused you to hunger for this level of surrender to your Lord Jesus, you can enter in through a fairly simple prayer. I submit the following prayer to you as a suggestion. You may pray whatever you like, but I urge you, in your prayer, to cover the essential points of my suggested prayer.

"Lord Jesus, I want to be baptized with your Holy Spirit. I want to be controlled and directed and empowered by Him, so that others are blessed and You are glorified. I confess that I have resisted Your Holy Spirit. I have had fear of man and selfishness, stubbornness, and willfulness. This is sin, and I repent of all of it.

"I declare bankruptcy on my old self-sufficient life, which has stifled the flow of Your Spirit in me. I hate that I have done this, and I renounce this old way, in Your Name, Lord Jesus. I ask You to forgive me for this sin. I receive Your forgiveness, with thanksgiving in my heart. I forgive myself. Now, I release my whole life into the control of Your Holy Spirit. Please baptize me in Your Holy Spirit; fill me and empower me for Your service. Take over, and run my life the way you want to run it.

"Please bring to maturity in my life the fruit of Your Holy Spirit. I want fullness of love, joy, and peace, and the rest of the fruit, not just for my blessing, but so that I may radiate Your presence before others, all to Your glory. Please use any of the gifts of Your Holy Spirit through me for the blessing of others. Give me the faith I will need to step out in these gifts. Direct me in learning about these gifts, so that I will be better prepared.

"I want to live the adventure of the supernatural life, serving you. I pledge, right now, that I will obey

Your nudges, trusting You to go before me to prepare the way for the ministry You want me to do. Thank You for the privilege of serving You in this way. Thank You for baptizing me with Your Holy Spirit. I pray all this in Your glorious Name, Lord Jesus. Amen."

If you prayed this prayer sincerely from your heart, you have begun the adventure of the supernatural life in Christ, empowered by the Holy Spirit. How does one get started serving the Lord in the supernatural life? As has been mentioned earlier, your availability is the starting place. It is a good idea to make yourself available to the Lord in a prayer early each day. That tends to help prepare us to be sensitive to other people and what is happening in their lives. In the Great Commandment, Jesus said we are to love our neighbors. These are not just the people who live next to us. Our "neighbors" are all the people whom God brings into our lives, including our family members.

Nearly every human living in this world has some kind of deep need that he cannot take care of through his own natural abilities. He longs for some supernatural solution to his need. Much of the Christian church has no answer for his need and tells him there is no answer beyond what he can do. So, he goes looking for his answer in drugs, alcohol, or even in the occult, where there really is supernatural power of the very wrong kind. Our Lord wants His disciples to show the world that He is supernatural and that He is willing to lovingly provide His supernatural power to meet the needs of people because He loves them. Your "neighbors" are looking for solutions to their needs, and you know the One who has the solutions.

Begin to pay attention to the neighbors who are in your life—at work, at the dry cleaner, in your social circle, in your church. Begin to observe their needs, and you will find that

God will give you insight, or discernment, about the needs of certain ones among your neighbors. Most people need more love than they are experiencing, especially God's *agape* love, unconditional love. Often, God begins to manifest His supernatural ministry through us simply by having us love someone in word and deed. This could involve finding ways to encourage the person whom God is causing you to notice. When this person feels God's love flowing from your heart, he or she may open up and share other needs.

When neighbors share needs, this gives us opportunities to offer to pray for them. When we are with one of these individuals, we should stay aware of the presence of the Holy Spirit and actively seek His guidance and empowering. Through our willingness to stay "tuned in" to the Holy Spirit concerning how to pray for the person, we may get direction that is different than what we expected. We also may be given an encouraging word to share with him. This encouraging word might even prove to be a prophecy.

When Philip was instructed by the Lord to leave his ministry in Samaria and go down to the road that led to Gaza, he did not know what an exciting surprise the Lord had in store for him. The Ethiopian whom he led to the Lord traveled on down to his native country with the Gospel flaming in his heart. He may have been the first Christian in Ethiopia, and he was a servant of the queen of Ethiopia. Our service to the Lord, when empowered and guided by the Holy Spirit, can bring amazing and unexpected blessings. God is about to do in your life more than you can ask or imagine (Ephesians 3:20).

CHAPTER FIFTEEN

Experiencing the Manifest Presence of God

Once we have become confident that God really is in control of His universe, that He loves and cherishes us, and that He is going to take care of us in a way that is really good for us, then we can trust Him enough to open up with real vulnerability and receive from Him. Our conviction is that Jesus is our perfect Shepherd who makes no mistakes, and we are His sheep, cared for in His pasture. He loves each one of us very passionately and very tenderly. He wants each of us to grow into strong, vibrant Christians who are His disciples, His witnesses, His warriors. His desire has always been to be "God with us" (see Matthew 1:23), and He has decided to accomplish that by living inside us in the Person of His Holy Spirit.

He loves living inside us, where He can know our thoughts and feel our feelings. He wants us to become comfortable with really deep intimacy with Him, trusting Him with those thoughts and feelings. We began our pilgrimage with Jesus by trusting Him with our eternity and with our daily lives. The Holy Spirit is the Spirit of Christ (Romans 8:9), and we can trust Him just as completely as we trust Jesus. He loves us just as Jesus loves us. Over the course of our lives, because He loves us He will lovingly bring about changes that we need in order to become what He has designed us to be. This will bring us great fulfillment and joy.

Because of the plan of the Godhead for Jesus to ascend to the Father, the Holy Spirit was given to us as the action Person of the Godhead here on earth. He carries out the will of Jesus our Lord and the ruler of the universe, and we can trust the Holy Spirit to act with the very same motives that Jesus has.

Jesus spoke to the issue of the trust His disciples had in Him when He said, "What man is there among you, when his son shall ask him for a loaf, will give him a stone? Or if he shall ask for a fish, he will not give him a snake, will he? If you then, being evil, know how to give good gifts to your children, how much more shall your Father who is in heaven give what is good to those who ask Him!" (Matthew 7:9–11). Jesus wants to establish in our hearts a very deep trust toward Him. This is in accord with Proverbs 3:5: "Trust in the Lord with all your heart, and do not lean on your own understanding."

We have good reason to trust that when we ask the Lord to minister to us by His Holy Spirit and to give us what He knows we need, that is what He will do, and He will protect us from possible attempts by the enemy to take advantage of our vulnerability before the Lord. He will give us all the discernment we need for our protection from the enemy in such a time of openness to the Holy Spirit. Too many Christians have a greater fear of being deceived by the enemy than they have a trust in the Lord to give them the discernment needed for their protection. They do not fully comprehend the very important and supernatural role that the Holy Spirit of God has in the lives of those who trust Him.

We have learned that our great God is omnipresent— that is, present everywhere. Sometimes He manifests His presence in ways that can be seen and felt, such as the time when He parted the Red Sea or when He healed the lame man at the gate of the temple, recorded in Acts 3:1–9. When we find ourselves in a worship service where the Lord has come in His "manifest presence," and we can sense or feel that He is there in power, this is an opportunity to receive ministry from Him. When we are having a time alone with the Lord—worshiping, reading, praying, and listening—we may sense His manifest presence. It may be in the form of His love washing over us, His power moving within us, or even a feeling of physical weakness as He comes to minister to us in deep ways.

When we recognize that He is present with us in His manifest presence, He knows that we know this. He is very interested to see how we will respond to this visit. Will we ignore Him, hoping He will go away? Will we act nonchalant or uninterested in His visit? Will we be polite and acknowledge His presence but not enter into intimacy with Him on this occasion? Or will we welcome Him with complete surrender to His presence, trusting Him in whatever He chooses to do with us or reveal to us during this visit?

In November 1970 I was still a "pre-Christian" and was being drawn by the Holy Spirit to the Lord Jesus. I wanted to read about Him, and one Saturday morning I was alone in the house while Carrie was at the store with our daughter Laura. I was just sitting in my favorite chair reading a book loaned to me by our pastor. Suddenly I felt the Lord's presence, and all my senses were quickened. I felt some fear, as I was sure that this was God and that I had angrily resisted Him in the past. It was clear that He had come to visit with me for some purpose. Then He began to talk to me audibly, in a deep voice that had real authority. He said several things to me, and by the time He had finished I had completely given up my driving need for autonomy and my resistance to His rule in my life. I had surrendered to God. Shortly thereafter

I prayed a prayer to surrender to the Lord Jesus and received Him as my Savior and Lord.

God is looking for our complete surrender. He cherishes our surrender and our trust in Him. It is part of who He wants us to become: surrendered disciples. He wants to develop in us complete trust and faith toward Him, so that we can be beneficiaries of the blessings that come from our obedience to His will and the blessing of peace that He gives us (see John 14:27 and Philippians 4:6–7). When we come to the place where we can be totally surrendered to Him whenever He comes in His manifest presence, then He can move upon us, in us, and through us to accomplish His purposes. His purposes may have to do with us, or He may lead us to minister to others, for their blessing.

If we are living in an attitude of carnal self-sufficiency, thinking we need nothing more from the Lord, we will probably not receive anything from Him. "God is opposed to the proud, but gives grace to the humble" (James 4:6). However, if we are living humbly before Him with an awareness of our great dependence upon Him, and we are hungry for His presence, we will most likely be able to receive from Him. This is a time for us to let down our "walls" and even allow ourselves to feel our love for Him emotionally.

People are usually hesitant to feel His love for them because they fear that they will have tears. We have been conditioned by our society to avoid crying, primarily because it is seen as a sign of weakness. In addition, most people feel out of control when they cry, and since they generally have a strong need to be in control, they don't want to cry. My view is that God gave us the ability to cry for a good purpose. After years of being in bondage to a fear of crying, I now cry readily when I'm being touched by the Lord and when I feel joy over something I am experiencing.

If a person is sitting in a comfortable chair, and the Holy Spirit comes in His manifest presence, it is good for him to surrender to what the Spirit has in mind. You can know with confidence that you will receive a blessing. As the Holy Spirit imparts to us what He has for us, we often will feel loved and very mellow, not wanting to move from that place. Some individuals who have had this experience numerous times describe it as "soaking in the presence of the Lord." Such times with the Lord are very beneficial to us.

There is a significant revival taking place across much of the world right now, and the Lord is doing some things that seem new to the current generation of Christians. He has been doing this "new thing" in the earth since the mid-90s. The Lord is showing up in His manifest presence in many meetings and church services on nearly every continent of the earth. The Holy Spirit is putting a hunger in Christians to receive directly from Him through the prayers of His faithful servants who are willing to remain after meetings and church services and pray for those who come forward. Typically, those who pray are the leaders, but others may pray as well. They are praying for the Holy Spirit to impart His blessing to seekers in ways that will meet their needs.

Scripture tells of a number of "new things" that the Lord has done. In the wilderness Korah led a revolt against Moses and Aaron, and God led Moses to demonstrate to the children of Israel that He planned to continue to use Moses as their leader. He had Korah and his group stand in front of their tents in the morning, as all Israel watched. Then Moses said, "By this you shall know that the Lord has sent me to do all these deeds; for this is not my doing. If these men die the death of all men, or if they suffer the fate of all men, then the Lord has not sent me. But if the Lord brings about an entirely new thing and the ground opens its mouth and swallows them up with all that is theirs, and they descend alive into Sheol, then you will understand that these men have spurned the Lord" (Numbers 16:28–30). In verses 31 and 32, we read that the earth opened up and swallowed up all of them. The Lord did an entirely new thing to fulfill His purposes.

Isaiah prophesied, "Do not call to mind the former things, or ponder things of the past. Behold, I will do something new, now it will spring forth; will you not be aware of it?" (Isaiah 43:18–19). He had prophesied in Isaiah 42:9, "Behold, the former things have come to pass, now I declare new things; before they spring forth I proclaim them to you."

Sending Jesus to take the sins of the world upon Himself on Calvary to become our Savior was certainly a new thing. The religious establishment could not receive this new thing. They had built their own worldview and theology and would have none of it. Then, to top it off, God decided to give His Holy Spirit to every true disciple of Jesus, to everyone who is born again. On the Day of Pentecost, Peter preached, "This is what was spoken of through the prophet Joel: 'And it shall be in the last days,' God says, 'that I will pour forth of My Spirit upon all mankind; and your sons and your daughters shall prophesy, and your young men shall see visions, and your old men shall dream dreams; even upon My bondslaves, both men and women, I will in those days pour forth of My Spirit and they shall prophesy' " (Acts 2:16–18). Again, God was doing a new thing.

As Saul (who was later called "Paul") was walking to Damascus (Acts 9:1–9), the Lord came to him in a flash of light. In the manifest presence of the Lord, Saul fell to the ground, overcome by the Lord's presence. The Lord Jesus was beginning a great work in Saul and took Saul's strength from him for a short time. This was a new thing.

When the Roman soldiers arrested Jesus in the garden, Jesus asked them, "Whom do you seek?" When they said, "Jesus, the Nazarene," He said to them, "I am He" (John 18:3–6). This was one of those special "I AM" moments, and the power of the Lord went forth from Him, and the soldiers all fell to the ground. Their strength failed them in

His manifest presence. This was another example of a new thing.

God's people have long engaged in the practice of clinging to what is familiar, because it feels safe. When God does a new thing, His people usually have a struggle with it. This new thing that God is doing, supernaturally meeting people's needs through the prayers of others for them, is somewhat unfamiliar territory for many Christians. Sometimes, in this ministry, the one being prayed for is overcome by the power of the Holy Spirit and consequently slumps to the floor. On the floor, he receives what God has for him. This may seem very strange to the more traditional Christian.

God's people are being set free from fears and anxiety, from deep wounds from the past, and they are being healed physically. This kind of prayer ministry is quite different from that which is commonly found in traditional church services. Not all churches engage in this type of ministry. This ministry occurs in churches whose leadership has decided to pursue what the Holy Spirit has for us. They have studied God's Word and have found that being baptized with the Holy Spirit is biblical and is a very important part of the Christian life. They have overcome the fear of the supernatural work of the Holy Spirit. They know that without His supernatural ministry to us and through us, we may remain trapped in our fears and be less effective in our service for the Lord.

During prayer ministry after a church service, the believers who are praying for individuals who are seeking the ministry of the Holy Spirit must have an attitude of complete surrender to the Holy Spirit, so that He can lead them in their ministry to the seekers. These intercessors must remain keenly attentive to ways that the Holy Spirit may lead them to pray. They may need to encourage the seekers to surrender to whatever the Holy Spirit wants to do during this time of prayer. They know that it is likely that some of the seekers for whom they pray will be overcome by the power of the Spirit and will rest in the Spirit on the floor, and that this will result in the seeker receiving from the Lord.

An increasing number of Christians are finding that they are able to receive ministry from the Holy Spirit in significant measure as they are alone in their homes or other quiet places. Many of them listen to worshipful music as they lie on the floor, a sofa, or even a bed, as they seek the Lord. As they surrender to the Holy Spirit's ministry, they acknowledge their dependence upon Him and let Him know what their needs are at that moment. Often they will invite Him to minister to other needs they may not have discerned yet, but that He knows about. The Holy Spirit has plans to minister to us in important ways for the duration of our lives here on earth. If we fail to give Him opportunities to minister to us, then less of that work will be accomplished in this lifetime.

In 1998, following a church service in which I had been ministering, a man came forward for prayer. He was in desperate condition emotionally. He was in his mid-forties and had just been told by his wife that she was divorcing him. Ten years earlier, this same situation had occurred with his first wife. After the first relationship failed, he had become a Christian, and he thought that divorce would never again occur in his life. When his second marital relationship failed, his heart was broken. The emotional pain was so great that he felt physical pain in his chest.

That night several of us gathered around him and prayed for him. The Lord's manifest presence came over him, and he slumped to the floor. The Lord knew that this gentleman needed to be on His "operating table." Like a comforting blanket, the peace of the Holy Spirit came over him. He soaked in the peace for about fifteen minutes. Then he began to cry. He cried for about fifteen minutes, as the Holy Spirit was at work healing his deep wounds. As the crying stopped, the peace came again for a while, and then he began to laugh.

He laughed really hard for about ten minutes. The Lord was restoring the joy of the Lord that had been stolen from him.

The peace came again for a while, and then he opened his eyes. He had been on the floor about forty-five minutes, and when he rose up from the floor he was completely healed. He could hardly believe it. All the pain was gone. He was ready to walk and leap and praise God like the man described in Acts 3:8 did. He has been filled with joy ever since.

Some Christians have trouble receiving from the Lord. They have two primary hindrances. The first hindrance is a habit of analyzing things too much. They think that if they can figure it out with their minds, they will be able to maintain control of it. The second hindrance is a desire to be in control so that, in their self-sufficiency, they can take care of themselves without any outside help. These brothers and sisters in the Lord do not realize that this attitude of self-sufficiency actually refuses God's involvement.

While a believer in this situation is being prayed for, to receive from the Holy Spirit, he is apt to be analyzing, asking a rapid series of internal questions such as "Is this what I'm supposed to be feeling? Is anything happening? Is anything going to happen? Is this person who is praying getting tired of praying for me?" In addition, as the presence of the Lord comes upon the person and he begins to feel a bit wobbly, his natural response is to do whatever it takes to maintain his composure, to stay in control. At that point he should just surrender all control to the Lord and yield to whatever the Lord is doing, trusting that the Lord knows best. This is a time to let our perfect Shepherd be in control, let Him impart right into our spirits whatever He wants, and let Him take care of us, as we consciously choose to trust Him without any reservations.

If we do all of the above, there is a pretty good chance that we will end up "resting in the Spirit" on the floor (others will catch us, and let us down gently). Then, if we maintain this surrender before the Lord while on the floor, as we lie there we will usually experience the wonderful peace that only the Holy Spirit can give. We mustn't begin analyzing while on the floor either. (What's happening now? Is anyone else on the floor? Am I in someone's way?) We should remain quiet and hungry for the Lord's presence, desiring to receive from Him in whatever way He chooses to minister to us. We may not feel anything but His peace, but we must not let that bother us. We can know that if He has put His peace upon us, He is at work in us in some way that is good for us. We may feel His power physically. He may heal hurts in our hearts, and this may cause us to cry. We should surrender to this crying. Just let the Lord do the healing that He has in mind. He may fill us with joy, so that we experience laughter. Let it flow! Enjoy it! Don't worry about anyone else around you.

The wonderful peace that the Lord grants at a time like this is a kind of spiritual anesthesia while He does things in our souls or our bodies. We should cherish this gift of His presence. We certainly can't manufacture it on our own. We should stay down on the floor as long as the Lord is pouring out the peace. Many people lie on the carpet (sometimes lovingly called "carpet time") for over an hour and never have a clue about what God is doing in their hearts. This is alright. You can be sure that He is doing something. That is why he put you down there on His operating table. However, some people experience a deep understanding of what He is doing. He knows when we need to know, and He knows when it's best for us not to know. Trust Him; He is trustworthy.

Men and women had similar experiences with the Holy Spirit during the Great Awakening in New England (1730–1760). During that time a leading Congregationalist pastor in Northampton, Massachusetts, Jonathan Edwards (1703–1758), wrote about the moving of the Holy Spirit among his church members. He was a solemn and careful preacher known for his sermon titled "Sinners in the Hands of an Angry God." When members of his church had some extraordinary experiences with the Lord, he diligently searched the Scriptures to gain understanding, and he prayed for Godly wisdom. His own wife, Sarah, was touched by the Holy Spirit in deep ways over a period of days. In her diary, she wrote,

> That night, 28 January, was the sweetest night I ever had in my life. I never before, for so long a time together, enjoyed so much of the light, and rest, and sweetness of heaven in my soul . . . with a continual, constant and clear sense of Christ's excellent and transcendent love, of His nearness to me and my dearness to Him; with an inexpressibly sweet calmness of soul in an entire rest in Him. . . . It seemed to be all that my feeble frame could sustain.

This testimony is recorded in *The Works of Jonathan Edwards*, by Jonathan Edwards, Edinburgh: The Banner of Truth Trust, 1992, Volume 1, page 65b.

God often has plans for us to meet with Him on His operating table several times, not just once. He uses these times to bring healing to the wounded places in our souls, and the Holy Spirit sometimes brings healing to our bodies. Oftentimes our minds are renewed as He reveals truth (see Romans 12:2); sometimes correction is given for our lives in order to mature us in Christ (see Colossians 1:25–29) or direction is given to move us into a specific area of ministry. During these times, the Lord usually will impart a greater measure of the anointing of His Holy Spirit, which empowers us for ministry to others.

Coming from His heart of love for us, the Lord wants to meet us where we are and meet our needs. He wants to help us with our relationships, with our finances, and with the wounds that we sustained as children and in our teenage years. He wants to free us from our hurts and from spiritual bondages and grow us into mighty men and women of God. One of the important ways He does this is by coming in His manifest presence and ministering to us by His Holy Spirit. He yearns for the day when we decide that we want this.

CHAPTER SIXTEEN

More Than We Can Imagine

We all need God's active involvement in our lives on a regular basis. We need His supernatural power operating in our lives if we are going to have any hope of becoming the church of Jesus Christ that He has in mind, which is much like the church that is described in the book of Acts. Christians often read the account in Acts 8 about Philip going to Samaria and ministering in supernatural power, casting out demons, leading scores to saving faith in Jesus, and ministering healing so that those who were paralyzed and lame were healed (Acts 8:7), and they think, "What they did back in those days is really exciting!" Then they close their Bibles and go about their non-supernatural lives, which they call "normal." They have difficulty imagining being personally involved in any such activity, so they don't even ask God to take them there.

Unlike the early Christian church, the current-day Christian church in the United States is permeated with the false idea that there is a scientific or natural explanation for what used to be considered a supernatural event. We have believed a lie.

I can remember when I was in seminary in the 1970s and the chairman of the New Testament Department of another major seminary was asked to speak to our student body; he was a well-known scholar at that time. He began his address by saying, "Let's get one thing straight, right away. No one walks on water unless it is frozen." He was attempting to debunk the "myth" that Jesus actually walked on water (Matthew 14:25). He considered himself a "modern" man who was above, or beyond, believing in supernatural things. He took the position that the miracles attributed to Jesus had been added to the story to enhance His image and thus help promote the Christian movement of the time. He held that there was no actual virgin birth of Jesus, etc., and he was teaching aspiring young pastors this point of view.

The truth is that God *is* supernatural. He really did create this universe by speaking it into existence, just exactly as the book of Genesis describes it. Since God created the universe, He can create anything He wants, whenever He wants. God has appointed His Son Jesus as King of the universe, over "all rule and authority and power and dominion, and every name that is named, not only in this age, but also in the one to come" (Ephesians 1:21).

It appears that because of the fallen nature of humanity and the condition of being separated from God (before we become Christians), we resist believing that God is supernatural. If we believed that He is supernatural, then *we would worship Him* instead of worshiping ourselves or rock stars. In this lost world, there is a strong resistance to believing that God does miracles or that He even does anything out of the ordinary. Instead, science declares that we live in a "closed universe" where everything is explainable in natural or scientific terms.

Only as we allow the Holy Spirit who lives in us to show us, do we begin to understand the supernatural. I have met large numbers of real, born-again Christians who still have trouble accepting the supernatural. I once heard it said, "When a believer sees his first real miracle with his own eyes, it usually changes his life." I think this is pretty well true. I do know that seeing a miracle is almost always a helpful experience for anyone. Faithful Christians don't need to see miracles all the time in order to live a wonderful, Spirit-filled life; however, seeing God do something supernatural sure does encourage us and keep our faith built up. In the thirty-seven years that I've been a Christian, I've seen many supernatural works of God, and I'm thankful for having seen every one of them.

Most of us grew up being taught that mankind descended from ape-like creatures and that this took millions of years. This teaching is properly called the theory of evolution. It came from a book titled *The Origin of the Species*, written by Charles Darwin, a scientist who lived in the nineteenth century. It seems to me that he had an urgent need to find an explanation for the origin of life that disagreed with the Bible's account of Creation.

Darwin's teaching has cast doubt on God's supernatural creative nature and His current-day involvement in the activities in the modern world. The unsaved world wants to believe that an individual human is the highest authority, unless he chooses to submit to another authority that he helped to put in place, such as a government. Unsaved man believes that since man cannot do supernatural things, the supernatural must not exist, except in fantasy.

Do we believe that God rescued His people from Egypt by parting the Red Sea so they could cross? When we read the whole fourteenth chapter of Exodus, we come face to face with the Word of God's account of one of the most wonderful miracles in history. Do we believe it? God saw to it that this record of His miraculous deliverance of His people from captivity in Egypt was preserved so that all of us can know the kind of supernatural, miracle-working, and loving God He is.

God does His miracles because He loves His people. As the people of Israel were trapped against the Red Sea, they were terrified as the chariots of Pharaoh closed in on them. They thought they were doomed. The idea that God would deliver them from this predicament was *more than they could even ask or imagine*. Moses, on the other hand, had faith to obey God and held his staff out over the waters and watched the miracle unfold.

As captain of the army of the King of Aram, Naaman was a proud and self-sufficient man. He also was a leper. Had it not been for his slave girl from Israel, he would have died of leprosy. However, she told him about a prophet in Israel named Elisha, who could bring healing to him. After a struggle with his pride, Naaman was finally able to seek out Elisha and receive healing from God (II Kings 5:1–14).

The Apostle Peter had been arrested, put in prison in Jerusalem, and was facing execution. The church was praying fervently for him. In answer to their prayers, God sent an angel to rescue him from prison. Peter's chains just fell off his hands, and when the angel led him to the gate that opened onto the street, the gate opened all by itself, and Peter was free. He went to the house where they were praying for him, and when the servant girl Rhoda heard his voice through the door, she told the others in the house that he was there, but they had trouble believing it was Peter. They had trouble believing that God could have done something as miraculous as setting Peter free from prison. They were able to *ask*, but they had difficulty *imagining* God doing it (Acts 12:5–17).

Paul was preaching at Troas (in a place now called "Turkey") late at night, and a boy who was sitting on a third-floor window ledge went to sleep and fell to his death. Paul went down and ministered to him and the boy was restored to life (Acts 20:7–12). God is in the miracle-working business because He loves His people. So, it is right for us to *ask* and then *imagine* that He will grant that which we have requested.

Missionaries Rolland and Heidi Baker have been on the mission field for twenty-five years. They are people who have surrendered their lives and their ministry to the Holy Spirit. Early in their ministry, they did not know about the blessing of being surrendered to the Holy Spirit. Instead, they had been encouraged to work very hard in their own strength and often worried about whether what they did would work.

They came to the place of surrender in 1995, and God began to do amazing things in their ministry in Mozambique, where some of the world's poorest people live. Starting with an orphanage with eighty children and no promised support, they prayed for God's miraculous provision. The number of children grew fairly quickly to more than three hundred, and they started a church in town, where hundreds received Jesus Christ as Savior and Lord. In addition, God healed many of the children from all manner of disease, in response to their prayers.

In the last ten years, their ministry has grown because of our miracle-working God. They now care for and feed more than two thousand children, and more than five thousand churches have been formed across Mozambique. They were able to ask and imagine. You can read about their ministry at: http://www.irismin.org/p/home.php.

About fifteen years ago, Ann, a thirty-five-year-old mother of two children who worked as a manager's assistant in an industrial warehouse, came to me very distraught. Her manager, a very tough woman, had asked her to lie to one of their suppliers in order to get a sample of their product at a very reduced price to use for display in the warehouse.

Ann was deeply concerned about doing something like that, since our Lord wouldn't approve. She also was concerned that if she refused to do it, she might be fired. "What do I do?" she asked.

I took her to Proverbs 29:25: "The fear of man brings a snare, but he who trusts in the Lord will be safe." I showed her that she feared what her boss would do; this is called "fear of man." I told her that God was saying that if she handled this right and trusted in him, she would be fine. I explained the principle of appealing to an authority instead of demanding rights and then suggested how she might express herself.

Then we prayed for her manager, according to Proverbs 21:1: "The king's heart is like channels of water in the hand of the Lord; He turns it wherever He wishes." We prayed, "Lord, you can turn the heart of a king, so surely you can turn the heart of Ann's boss. We ask you to touch her heart and work this out, in Jesus' name."

The next day Ann said to her boss, "I'm feeling really uncomfortable about telling them that this unit was damaged in shipping, so that we can use it as a display and pay only 10% of its worth."

Her boss responded, "Yeah, I don't know what I was thinking. Just forget about it. I'll think of something else."

About twelve years ago, I was invited to "preach a weekend" at a small church in North Carolina. This meant I would preach Friday night, Saturday night, Sunday morning, and Sunday night. I also scheduled counseling appointments during the day on Saturday.

In prayer I began to seek the Lord about what He wanted me to preach during those four services. I was feeling really good about how the preparation was going until the Thursday before the weekend, when the pastor called to tell me that he had invited a music group to minister on Friday night, to sort of "kick off the weekend."

"Dick, that means you only have to preach three times, and you still get to minister after the music on Friday night." Well, he hadn't considered that normally I pretty much count on my message to set the stage for the ministry time at the end of the service. I thought to myself, "Oh, great, now I get to minister without any preparation of the congregation. Hmmm." I felt pretty uneasy about that. God was not even a little uneasy about it.

As I sat in the congregation during the ministry of the music group on Friday night, I was aware of how wonderful their ministry was. I could feel the presence of the Lord very strongly. What a blessing it was. Their leader had planned to take up the offering for his group at the end of their ministry. Instead, he stood there for a moment feeling the very strong presence of the Lord, and then he looked at me and said, "Pastor Robinson, this is no time to take up an offering. This is the time for you to minister. Would you come on up, please?"

I walked up on the platform excited about the presence of the Lord that I sensed, but I didn't know how to begin ministry with those people. I didn't know anyone there except the pastor. On this occasion, my *imagining* wasn't working very well, and so I hadn't been *asking*. All I could do was to quietly say, "Help, Lord."

Within seconds, the Lord gave me a word of knowledge (I Corinthians 12:8), which I spoke out immediately: "There is a mother here who is estranged from her teenaged daughter. This estrangement has been going on for several years, and it is breaking your heart. The devil has been pounding on you, telling you what a terrible mother you have been. The Lord says you have not been a terrible mother. He says you have been a good mother, and He wants you to come forward and receive the blessing He has for you."

When I began giving that word, almost everyone in the place turned and looked at Susan. Her head went down somewhat as she began to weep. I could tell which one she was when I looked in the direction where everyone was looking.

When I said the Lord wanted to bless her, she began to wail loudly as she got in touch with her pain. She charged forward to the steps of the platform and fell to her knees, still crying loudly. I met her at the steps, as God allowed me to feel some of her pain in my own heart. I prayed out loud, "O God, she has had such wounding pain. Would You please heal her heart and replace that pain with Your peace." I laid my hand on her head.

Within about fifteen seconds, she was silent and at peace. I waited upon the Lord. Then came another word of knowledge, and I prayed, "Oh, God, she has had her joy stolen from her for this whole time. Please restore her joy to her. Give her Your joy." Almost immediately, she began to laugh, loudly. It seemed a bit odd at the time, until I remembered how laughter brings such healing to our souls. She laughed for about five minutes, and then just knelt there in peace, with a smile on her face, basking in the Lord's love and affirmation.

I left her with the Lord as I invited others to come forward for prayer. God continued to work in amazing ways among those precious people. In this case, at first I was neither *imagining* nor *asking* very well, but God could see that my heart was willing and eager to be used for the blessing of His people, so He gave me those words of knowledge to bless Susan and to edify His people. As the ministry time went on, God continued to do supernatural things with His people, blessing and nurturing them.

That same weekend, on Sunday morning, I preached on the availability of the peace of Jesus and how much we need that, from John 14:27: "Peace I leave with you; My peace I give to you; not as the world gives, do I give to you. Let not your heart be troubled, nor let it be fearful." I explained that our natural way is to want to control our own circumstances so that things will go well for us. However, we are very much not able to control these things, and this leaves us stressed and deprived of the peace of Jesus. We can very easily live our entire lives all tied up in knots, deprived of the peace of Jesus, living in the flesh. I explained that our Lord wants to give us His peace, that it is a fruit of the Holy Spirit, and that we just need to give Him control and the peace will come.

As I was preaching, a man in his thirties got up and began pacing back and forth across the back of the sanctuary, glowering at me. What I was saying appeared to be upsetting him. He tried to sit down twice but couldn't. He kept pacing. When I concluded my message, I gave an invitation: "Any who recognize that you very much need the peace of Jesus and you want it right now, please come on down front, and I will pray for you. Jesus is willing to impart His peace to you right now."

The man who had been pacing came striding down the aisle where I was standing. As he came near, I could see that he had tears in his eyes and his lips were quivering. I knew that the Holy Spirit was working in him in a strong way. The Holy Spirit was showing me that he had been trying with all his might to hold his life together in his own strength and that he was near a breaking point.

When he arrived in front of me, tears were streaming down his face. I gently grasped him by his upper arms, looked in his eyes, and said, "What is your name?"

He said, "Rodney."

I said, "Are you ready to give it up, Rodney?"

He said, with a sob, "Yes."

I simply instructed him to tell the Lord, "I give it up."

When he said those words to the Lord, through his tears, the Holy Spirit instantly responded to his cry for help and began imparting a great anointing of His peace into Rodney. He slumped to the floor, overcome by the love and power of the Holy Spirit. I knelt beside him, placed my hand on his chest, and asked the Lord to release him from all his striving, install faith in him so he could trust the Lord, and then fill him with His supernatural peace. Rodney's wife had now arrived beside him, and I asked her to stay with him, because he was probably going to be there for quite a while. She agreed. He was on the floor for an hour and a half, while the Holy Spirit did some really deep work in him.

In the church service that night, I asked Rodney to testify about what God had done in his life. He testified that he had never been able to feel the Lord before because of how uptight and stressed he was. That morning he had felt the power of the Lord come upon him, and when he was lying on the floor he had been enveloped in God's peace. He said that now he was filled with peace and a strange new joy. He said the Lord spoke to him and told him that He would always be there for him, so he could stop all his worrying. He told Rodney that as he walked in the peace that God was installing in him, he was now going to be able to grow into a mighty man of God. When Rodney said that last part, he grinned broadly.

When I gave the invitation for people to come forward to receive the peace of Jesus, I had confidence that He would impart His peace to any who came forward. During that time of ministry, several others received His peace much as Rodney had received it. After my own initial struggle with being able to imagine and then ask for such a thing, God showed me that He would be faithful to fill His people with His peace, since it was His will to touch those who hunger for His peace and surrender to it. Now I can give that invitation with a great deal of faith and confidence. The Lord has taught me how to ask and imagine. Praise the Lord.

In recent times, the Lord has been working at expanding my own ability to ask and imagine, especially in the area of praying for the physical healing of His people. I have had confidence in praying for emotional healing and in ministering deliverance from evil spirits. However, there has been some kind of inner hesitancy in my faith for physical healing. As a result of that hesitancy, I had seen less than two dozen physical healings during thirty years of praying for people. I have been disappointed in this lack of results.

Recently, God has been increasing my faith in this area, and I have seen Him move in healing. A woman in her fifties had very badly bruised or broken ribs that brought substantial pain to her. She could hardly move her upper body without experiencing pain. She asked for prayer for healing. After reading James 5:14–16 over her and anointing her with oil, I prayed a simple prayer for her healing. I told her how Jesus had ministered to a blind man and then had asked him, "Do you see anything?" The man had responded that he saw men like trees walking. (Jesus had been checking to see how the healing was going.) The man had responded that he could see something, but that he could not see clearly. Jesus then ministered to him some more, and the man had been completely healed (Mark 8:22–25).

After I had prayed, I asked the woman with the bruised ribs, "Please turn your upper body all the way to the left." She did, and then she exclaimed, "It doesn't hurt!" I asked her to turn to the right, and she said the same thing. I asked her to hold both arms straight up above her head. She did, and exclaimed, "This doesn't hurt either!" Then she knew that her Lord Jesus had healed her, and she jumped to her feet and began praising God.

Not long ago, a woman in her sixties came for a scheduled time of ministry for inner healing. She got out of her car with a cane and walked very slowly from my driveway, up the steps, and into my home, obviously in pain. She sat in the chair I provided for her, and she laid her cane on the floor by the chair.

God did some wonderful healing in her soul that day as she surrendered her entire life to Him, and she felt the Lord's peace like never before. At the conclusion of our meeting, in preparation to leave, she bent over and picked up her cane and then bounded to her feet and strode through my house, holding the cane in its middle. She had entered my house in pain, but now it was gone. She quickly went down my steps to the driveway and bounded to her car with her cane held above her head, giving praise and thanksgiving to God. This was a time when I didn't even specifically pray for physical healing, yet God in His sovereign love and mercy chose to heal her body. Praise His Name!

God has not ceased His supernatural ministry in this world. He is still moving across the earth in His sovereign power and with love in His heart for His people. He wants to bless His people and also many who are not yet Christians. Jesus said, "I have other sheep, which are not of this fold; I must bring them also, and they shall hear My voice; and they shall become one flock with one shepherd" (John 10:16). Jesus is looking for people who will allow His Holy Spirit to move through them to do the works that Jesus did when He walked on this earth (see John 14:12).

CPSIA information can be obtained
at www.ICGtesting.com
Printed in the USA
LVOW12s1215060717

540419LV00001BA/149/P